The Bare Bones
Book of Screenwriting

*The definitive beginner's guide to
story, format and business*

By J.T. Clark

D1714470

WBC, Publishing
P.O. BOX 11714
Newport Beach, CA 92658
(323) 447-9676
jthomasclark@gmail.com
www.barebonesscreenwriting.com

First edition

BISAC: PER004050   PER004000   PER019000

ISBN-13: 978-0-9795102-0-5

ISBN-10: 0-9795102-0-1

E-BOOK ISBN-13: 978-0-9795102-1-2

Library of Congress Control Number: 2007901125

CONTENTS

CHAPTER II:
WRITING THE SCREENPLAY
The Only Thing You Can't B.S.: 35

CHAPTER III:
BUSINESS
A medieval mentality: 69

CHAPTER ZERO: GETTING STARTED

"The easiest thing to do on earth is not write."

William Goldman

Winning the Hollywood "jackpot" has lured everyone, their mothers, their uncles, and their local taxman into the business of writing and selling screenplays. Most people will predictably shell out some time and money, not see results and then quit playing the game. Or, there are addicts; those who continually lose by doing the same thing, making the same mistakes, over and over again. They trudge forward like foolish soldiers wasting, in some cases decades, other life opportunities—and possibly many marriages—while hoping one day to reach that golden ticket that does not exist.

This guide is intended for the other type of writer: the writer who desires a professional career writing feature films and is willing to learn, and work, to build it brick by painstaking brick.

THE WRITER AS OBSERVER

As a writer, it is your responsibility to know how people talk, act, react and interact. It is your job to be able to describe details in any given situation. Start taking a notepad around with you. Jot ideas as they come. Take notes from an interesting exchange of dialogue you overhear in a restaurant. Look at an image and try to describe it textually. Become aware; a constant observer.

TIP: *A tape recorder is a good idea. Also, buy a stack of yellow legal pads to always have one on hand. Keep one in your car too.*

ABSORB EVERYTHING

"Boring person = boring writer"

Be a student of life. If you aren't an interesting person you won't be an interesting writer. Watch Discovery Channel. Read the newspaper. Take odd jobs. Meet people you ordinarily wouldn't meet. Talk to them. Ask questions. Go places you wouldn't usually go. Take classes. Take vacations. Live life! Good writers, directors and actors are like sponges: they absorb life experiences and apply them to their craft.

In the end, what separates your writing voice from the rest of the writers are your experiences as a human being, your talents and how these things inform your words.

READ, READ, READ

When you start to read a ton of scripts, you'll start to "get" the lingo, style and format of the screenplay. You can use techniques other writers use to help you in certain situations. Read good scripts to see what works. Read bad scripts to see what doesn't. Watch a movie and have the script in front of you to read along with it. (NOTE: Not all published scripts are identical to a completed edited film.) Watch for similarities or differences between the script and the film.

REFERRAL: www.script-o-rama.com is a great online resource for downloading screenplays for free!	HABIT: read the trades to know what's up in the industry. The top trades are "The Hollywood Reporter" and "Variety"	RECOMMENDED BOOKS: Robert McKee's, "STORY" and William Goldman's "Which Lie Did I Tell?"

WATCH MOVIES

Don't feel guilty. It's homework. Watch them once for fun, then a second time to study and take notes. Get a Netflix account—you're gonna spend a lot more time in front of the boob-tube now that you have a legitimate excuse for being a couch potato.

DEVELOP A SCHEDULE AND JUST WRITE

Most writers do not like to write. Make a schedule, and it doesn't matter what that schedule is. Some writers write a certain number of words a day. Some writers write a certain number of pages a day. And some write a certain number of hours a day. As long as you're writing you're on the right track.

Even if you are not inspired, once you sit down your brain will crack open. Don't spend your energy thinking that you're wasting your time by not earning money from the start. There is a reward involved. It just may not be until years down the road; the effort is an investment that can pay off. If it helps, pay yourself. Put a dollar amount on your worth per hour, and stuff that into a jar.

> **TIP:** *If you write one script page per day, you will have a first draft screenplay in three months!*

YOUR CONCEPT

Finding your concept is the first step to writing a screenplay. Make sure it's an idea that you want to commit to. Remember, you may spend months, or even years, on one single concept—so you have to be attached to it. I can't tell you how to select a concept. It could come from a character, an article, an event, memory, a joke—anywhere.

Make sure your concept is not already a book or movie, or that your version is in some way unique. *(More about using copyright material and life rights in Chapter 3: Business.)*

Once you have committed to an idea, write it in one or two sentences. Look at it. Hold it in your hand. Is the idea worthy of a two-hour movie, or is it better suited for a short story, a novel, a short film, a comic book or a poem?

Movie concepts involve characters, usually a main character at the center of it, with conflicts and goals. Movies are *visual*. Some story ideas—although appealing—just cannot be crafted into a movie. Pitch your concept to friends, family, and other people whose opinions you trust, and judge their reactions.

Hollywood typically makes high concept movies. **High concept** refers to a concept that can usually be pitched in one sentence with high marketability and franchise power. "Jurassic park", "Rocky", "Indiana Jones"," James Bond", "Friday the 13th"are all high concept films.

YOU'D BETTER HAVE CONFLICT!

Conflict is what drives story. If you don't have conflict in a story, you're not writing a movie. Conflict to screenwriting is like musical notes to a piece of music. Conflict moves a story forward as notes push a song forward. Whatever your main character's goal is, it should be *near impossible* to achieve. Around every corner there should be forces working against him/her to ensure failure.

There's an old Hollywood saying about conflict: *"Throw your character up in a tree…and then throw rocks at him."*

KNOW YOUR GENRE

Unless you're writing an experimental film, you need to know what type of movie you are writing from the get-go. Why? Form. Rules. *And* business. Yes, I know, you're just a writer. Well, if you want to stay *just* a writer (as in writing in the corner of your room…alone) you're going to have to think about the business aspects of screenwriting. From a business standpoint, genre is very important.

Genre Films are groups of films where each film in that group has an instantly recognizable pattern: like setting, subject matter, theme, mood, period, plot, narrative events, motifs (explained later), style, structure, situations and recurring icons.

Viewers expect a certain set of criteria when they pay to view a genre film. Readers, agents, producers, investors and actors expect that same set of criteria if they are to be involved with a script. Most writers get very good at one genre before venturing into other genres. They *niche* themselves.

Think of business: If you need a carpenter for a specific job, you will think to yourself, "Joe does cabinetry. But I need to get Timmy because *he* does granite." The same concept goes for Hollywood. No one will hire a drama writer to write a comedy unless he's proven himself at comedy. Even then, it can be tough to convince a studio to give that writer a chance.

GENRES: *Action, Adventure, Comedy, Crime/Gangster, Drama, Epic/Historical, Horror, Musical, Science Fiction, War, Westerns.*	**SUB-GENRES:** *Biographical Films, "chick" flics, Detective/Mystery, Disaster, Fantasy, Film Noir, Guy Films, Melodramas, Road Films, Romance, Sports, Supernatural, Thrillers.*

Many films combine genres or sub-genres while some genres have several different categories. Take the comedy genre for example, which can have sub-categories, including: Black Comedy, Schtick, Romantic Comedy, Satire, Spoof.

Find out what genre you are writing for. Do your research and know the rules of the game before you get on the field. Watch movies and read scripts.

RESEARCHING

Create a separate file for each story. Research can be done in many ways: at the library, on the Internet, with magazines and newspapers. But firsthand research is always the best. When you can get close to your material by interviews, pictures and conversations it's a lot stronger and will spark brainstorms. If you are writing a sports story, try to interview an athlete or coach or fan. If you are writing a horror film, go scout locations and take a camera for inspiration.

TIP #1: *Enjoy the many different aspects of screenwriting, because lets face it, sitting down and writing can be just plain boring.*

TIP #2: *If you see a particular actor fitting a role in your story, cut a picture out of a magazine and tack them on the wall to give you a visual.*

DEVELOP YOUR CONCEPT

Development is a complicated idea. It's the culmination of character development, plotting, themes, tones and story. It's tough to juggle. You need to get the idea into your head, and accept it, that things will change. You really need to get used to trashing bad material. Letting go of ideas that don't work is healthy and encouraged. Be adaptable. Never expect anything you write to stay the way you first wrote it. That being said, penmanship and grammar are not important right now. Ideas and organization is what matters.

To get started, I suggest using a simple breakdown method to give you an overall view of your project. This will take the concept out of your head and put it onto paper. This will be your movie in a one-page view including the **title, genre, tone, era, budget and logline**. After you've completed this exercise, hang this one sheet of paper on the wall at your work area.

Title: Make a list of possible titles. This doesn't have to be decided upon until much, much later but get the ball rolling now. Titles usually involve a character name, a theme, a setting, a saying, an event or a mood from your story.

Genre: Pinpoint your genre and stick to the rules of that style.

Rating: By giving your movie a rating (i.e., G, PG, PG-13, R, etc.) it will allow both you and readers to grasp it better. At the end of the day the writer doesn't determine the rating, but having a clear idea of the type of movie you are writing is a good thing.

Tone: Tone is the hardest element to convey through a screenplay, and it is easily misinterpreted. Try and pinpoint the tone of your movie by relating it with other films. Examples: My movie is a cross between *National Lampoon's Vacation* and *Parenthood*. Or: *Goodfellas* crossed with *Nightmare on Elm Street*.

Era: Know what time period your story takes place in. New writers should steer clear of period pieces and epics because they usually require huge budgets. *(More about writing the wrong spec scripts in Chapter 3: Business.)*

Budget: Determine the general budget for your movie. The smaller your budget, the faster your script will be made or sold as a new writer. I encourage all new writers to write small films.

> Micro budget (0 to 100k)
> Low budget (100k to 5 million)
> Medium budget (5 to 20 million)
> Big budget (20 million +)
> *King Kong, 2005* (205 million)

Logline: A logline is a one sentence "pitch" of your story. It is the movie-concept communicated quickly and clearly. To construct a logline, think of how you would tell a friend about your film in just one sentence while at a party. It should include **who** the story is about (protagonist) **what** he/she strives for (goal) and **who/what** is standing in the way (antagonistic force) of accomplishing this goal.

Example:

E.T. Logline: *An alienated boy bonds with an extraterrestrial child who's been stranded on earth; the boy defies the adults to help the alien contact his mother ship so he can go home.*

ORGANIZATIONAL METHODS

Keeping track of all your files, notes and ideas can be overwhelming during the story process. A good method, whether using a computer or not, is to **create several folders**: One for characters; One for story and treatment; One for the script; One for dialogue notes. This will help you locate information at any given time instead of digging around, losing writing momentum.

ORGANIZATIONAL TIP #1:
Write scenes on flashcards so you can re-arrange them for structure. Use a corkboard on a wall to keep everything in view.

ORGANIZATIONAL TIP #2:
Use butcher paper to write your story on. Roll it out and see the film as it happens. You can also hang the butcher paper on your wall to diagnose structure problems or write notes, draw pictures or tack up research.

CHAPTER I: STORY IS KING

Staple it to Your Forehead

Without a good story, you will not have a good script, regardless of brilliant dialogue, amazing characters or kick-ass fight scenes.

Without a good story, the entire chain of events that must successfully align during the process of making a movie will fall apart before your very eyes. It's nearly impossible to get a good, or even just a decent, actor, agent, director or producer to attach themselves to a bad or even mediocre story. Even your own film crew will be hesitant about working on a bad story. No one wants his or her name on a film audiences will boo at, or never watch—unless there's major cash involved. Don't get me wrong – there's nothing wrong with major cash being involved.

Remember: take your time. Don't rush the story process. It's a tricky balance of craft and creativity, building character, plot, theme and subplots into a seamless, logistical sequence that leads to a cathartic resolution.

WHO? WHY? WHAT? HOW? WHEN? WHERE?

To start your story process, start asking questions. Think of yourself as an intrepid archeologist trying to dig up and reveal to the world the story you have deep inside you. When ideas pop into your head, think of it as a starting point. When you ask yourself questions, you will find many interesting paths to go down, or many ideas to ditch that do not work.

THINK OPPOSITE: Think opposite. It's crazy, but sometimes you will find the best solution if you think opposite. What do I mean by opposite? For example, let's say you have a character that you think is kind-hearted. Think opposite. Maybe this character is kind-hearted for the most part, except he/she is cruel to animals. This makes for a more interesting character, and some doggie kicking scenes that will surprise/shock your audience. Or, let's say you think of an idea for a location: a park. Think opposite. What would happen if that location were a nuclear power plant? You just turned a boring romantic comedy into something interesting.

THE SYNOPSIS

A synopsis is a short summary of your story. It should articulate a genre, tone, setting, mood, main characters and conflicts. It's a snapshot of your story—but more expanded than a logline. Think a paragraph rather than a sentence. A synopsis doesn't need to contain every detail, or give away the ending, but it should entice your audience to read the entire script. You know the little blurb on the back of every movie cover in the video store? Well, that's a synopsis. It's mainly a marketing tool. But you need one sitting in front of you to know your story.

Alfred Hitchcock once said that he first liked to look at his film as a concept—something he could hold in his hand, juggle around and play with. He liked to expand that concept into one sheet of paper. He then liked to develop that one page into a ten-page treatment before writing the script.

Story is a process, step by step, one step at a time. You cannot go from the concept to the script, unless you want a headache.

FUN FACT: *"Shrek" was pitched, and sold to executives on one piece of paper. This is an example of how much leverage a strong synopsis can generate.*

Sample Synopsis

Robert Altman's "The Player"

A sleek and smooth Hollywood studio executive starts receiving death threats from a disgruntled writer because he has committed the ultimate Hollywood sin—he promised the writer he would call him back and he never did. This is particularly ironic because the studio executive, Griffin Mill , is considered "writer-friendly," spending his days listening to pitches from such noted screenwriters as Buck Henry, who is pushing "The Graduate, Part II" and Alan Rudolph, who is hawking a Bruce Willis action film described as "Ghost meets The Manchurian Candidate." But The Player finds Griffin's comfortable lifestyle in danger of collapse. He is trying to find a way to unload his girlfriend whose independence and intelligence make her a poor candidate for a trophy wife. More importantly, it seems that Larry Levy, a slippery executive from 20th Century Fox, is angling for his job. And then there are those nasty postcards and faxes from a screenwriter threatening to kill him.

("Synopsis: The Player." January 2nd, 2007, http://movies.aol.com/movie/the-player/6330/synopsis)

THE BEAT SHEET

Sometimes referred to as a "step outline" a beat sheet is an optional development tool for the writer, but has proven to be successful in organization and story development. It is the process of breaking your story down into manageable "beats" before you write the outline or treatment. Typically with a beat sheet you end up with four or five pieces of paper with 20 to 30 steps outlining the major story points of your script.

Number or letter the beats. The point is to see your entire story within a few pages. This exercise will crack your story open for further development. You don't need to be extremely detailed. You'll find plenty of holes to fill in later. Just write the major scenes and points of the story that will drive it from beginning to end. You only need a sentence or two for each beat. Like this:

1) Skate Park. We meet TOM and his friends.
2) Tom's house. His parents are fighting. He goes to his room.
3) Tom's friend calls him to invite him to a party. There will be drugs.
4) Party. Tom is peer pressured into smoking pot.

THE TREATMENT a.k.a. THE OUTLINE

A treatment is an expanded and developed version of the synopsis, complete with: plot, subplots, characters and most scenes. This is <u>not</u> a teaser. The treatment, or outline, must be thoroughly developed and will be used not only as a guide to help you write the screenplay but also as a marketing tool for your screenplay to get actors, agents and producers interested in your script.

A good outline should read somewhat like a short story, written with prose. It should contain a fair amount of details but overloading it with camera angles and such overly detailed information isn't recommended, and should be saved for the script.

You can start your treatment anytime. But it is always a work in progress. Be prepared to get messy, treatments are ugly during the development stage. Think of the process as slinging mud on the wall to see what sticks. When things stick, develop on it. When they don't, remove them. It doesn't matter what order of the story you work on in a treatment. It's normal to write the ending when you don't have a middle. It's okay to jump around and fill in blanks.

ADVICE: *It's easier to fix problems in a treatment than a script. Those writers who dash off scripts over a weekend poolside will have a sloppy mess. Not a product.*

FUN FACT: *At a discussion forum at USC, Mark Romanek, writer/director of "One Hour Photo", which starred Robin Williams, claimed he wrote the script in three weeks. Well, what he didn't tell his audience was that he probably spent months, if not years on the treatment.*

TIPS: *A typical outline will run 6 to 12 pages. But there is no standard length. I prefer using single spaced paragraphs. You can label the acts if it makes things easier. Capitalize characters as you introduce them. It's okay to write minimal dialogue, but keep it short.*

CHARACTER BACKSTORY

It's vital that you know the backstory of your main characters and world *before* starting your script. A backstory is information concerning character and world prior to the beginning of the story. You may not need 90% of the backstory, but it will give you reference points along the way for characterization, plotting and dialogue. Knowing this information will help you understand how you got to your starting point.

Here are some categories to develop backstory:

- **Convictions and beliefs:** A Buddhist, Christian and Atheist will each lead very different lives. Figure out your characters' belief system(s); why they have them and what experiences they've had with them that have shaped their lives.
- **Era:** Are we in the 80s? The 90s? The future? The past? What social perspectives are at play for your setting?
- **Education:** Formal? Non-formal? Is your character a dropout or a genius? Street smart or book smart? If they went to college, which one and why? And what was their experience like?
- **Family background:** Family has a lot to do with character. Dig into your characters' pasts and learn about their surroundings, influences and social status.
- **Geographic location:** A character that grew up in New York will be much different than one who grew up in Los Angeles or Paris. Take into account culture, expectations, climate, economy, language and accents. This will play into a character's view on all the little things, like sports, food, clothing, values and interactions.
- **Past successes and failures:** Success and failures can shape a character for life. Find your character's successes as well as failures to learn why he/she acts the way they do in certain situations today.
- **Phobias:** Learn what your characters are afraid of. And make sure they have to face it in your story. For example: the film "Arachnophobia" was fueled by the main character's fear of spiders.

- **Profession:** It's a no-brainer that a carpenter and a chemist have different personalities. What does your character do for a living? Find a fitting occupation, or an occupation that goes against the character. If you have a very rigid character, they won't want to be working in a porn shop. But that's a great place to put them.
- **Quirks:** Does your character have O.C.D.? Do they have allergies? Are they picky with food? Do they like to sleep with two pillows or enjoy being licked on the hand by a dog? Details and quarks add up. The film "A Beautiful Mind" tackles one man's battle with schizophrenia. A character's quirks can propel your story forward.
- **Values:** We all have values. Where did your character get them? Do they like their values? What do they value? Money? Animals? Love? Work? Honesty?
- **Talents:** Discover what natural talents your characters have and let it play into the story. Maybe they never knew they could play guitar. Maybe they are athletic by nature. Or maybe they have special skills in the bedroom, if you know what I mean.

PLOT DEFINED

A plot is the arrangement of events in a narrative, which, traditionally, includes five elements:

Conflict: the antagonist and protagonist of the story are described
Exposition: past details leading up to the conflict are revealed
Rising Action: the events leading to the climax
Climax: the "turning point" for the protagonist
Resolution: resolution of the conflict

CLASSICAL STRUCTURE

You gotta know the rules before you can break them

In short, structure is the placement of scenes in a particular, logistical order. The simpler your structure is the better your audience will understand your story, and the easier time you'll have selling it.

Because this is a manual for beginning to intermediate screenwriters, I focus only on the three act, "linear structure" (classical structure) because it is the foundation for storytelling, past, present and future. There really is nothing new under the sun except depletion of our ozone.

In classical Hollywood linear structure every event advances the narrative forward. All characters act as causal agents for the narrative. Classical structures also use familiar images, expressions, archetypal characters and symbols to relate the story to the audience.

William Goldman (writer of "Butch Cassidy and The Sundance Kid") describes a successful screenplay as being constructed of several scenes strung along a single thread. All scenes connect and represent something. They are all related and each pushes the film forward by information or character.

If you find a scene that does not fall along this "spine" of your screenplay, it must be cut. You will trash much more material than you will use. It might not feel like it at first, but that's a good thing.

The best way to learn this structure is to study films and break them down.

THE THREE-ACT STRUCTURE EXPLAINED

"People have forgotten how to tell a story. Stories don't have a middle or an end anymore. They usually have a beginning that never stops beginning."

Steven Spielberg

All stories have a beginning, middle and end—not necessarily placed in that order. I strongly suggest a first-time writer to steer clear of writing non-linear structure (the movies "Pulp Fiction" and "Memento" are prime examples), as you will not learn nearly as much about writing. It is best to learn the basics and the rules before you expand on the rules and break them. But if you're headstrong, then go for it. Study up on films with non-linear structure and read the scripts.

Let me break down tradition structure:

Act 1: The Set Up. Your main character (protagonist) identifies a quest or goal, and an obstacle (the antagonist—which doesn't necessarily have to be "a person"), and sets a deadline for his or her goal.

Act 2: The Confrontation. The protagonist faces obstacles while getting closer toward the goal. Each obstacle is increasingly more difficult leading to a point where the goal seems unobtainable (sometimes called in the business "the black cave"). The protagonist and antagonist face one another in the climax.

Act 3: The Resolution. Protagonist achieves the goal, or doesn't, or succeeds at great cost.

A VISUAL EXAMPLE OF STRUCTURE

Here's a good general snapshot of screenplay structure if we could look at it like a scientist. The squiggly lines represent **rising tension.** The 'Y' axis is the level of tension, as the 'X' axis is the measure of time. I added an *approximate* page count to illustrate a timeline.

Page count: 1   15   30   45   60   75   90   105

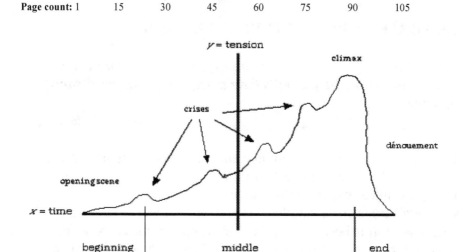

("Structure and Plot." February 11th, 2007 http://www.musik-therapie.at/PederHill/Structure&Plot.htm)

ACTS, SEQUENCES, SCENES, BEATS
The Building Blocks of a Script Broken Down

A classically structured screenplay is comprised of three acts. *Act One* is typically 15 to 30 pages; *Act Two* is typically 50 to 60 pages; and *Act Three is* typically 10 to 30 pages.

- **Acts are broken up into sequences**, which can each run 12 to 15 pages.
- **Sequences are broken up into scenes**, which can each run 2 to 6 pages.
- **Scenes are broken up by beats**, which are comprised of action and dialogue.

A well-crafted screenplay will typically run 100 to 130 pages, have three acts, 12 to 18 sequences and 30 to 40 scenes.

Personally, I don't prescribe to the paint-by-numbers recipe for screenwriting like some books teach, but I am a believer in conventions, rules and knowing what has worked in the past and what continues to work today.

Don't feel completely walled in if your story's scene or sequence numbers are far off the charts. The numbers above are simply to be used as a guide to work from. It's a template in order to steer you in a generally solid direction regarding structure and form.

ANALOGY: *Think of a screenplay as building a house. You must first build the outside walls (acts) then interior walls (sequences) and then fill the house out with cabinets, furniture, lights, surfacing, flooring, etc. (scenes, beats, dialogue). If you mess up on the exterior walls, then you will have to tear everything down within those walls. This is why it is very important to spend time writing and re-writing the treatment, which sets up the blueprints for the house structure.*

THE HERO'S JOURNEY

The hero's journey is an archetypal layout of structure and patterns found in most stories, past, present and future. These are patterns that are as ancient as man himself.

> **ADVICE:** *Go to the library and spend some time reading Joseph Campbell's "Hero with a Thousand Faces" and Aristotle's "Poetics" for some "old school" tips and tricks on story structure and character.*

Below is the Hero's Journey summarized. To paint a better picture and relate these patterns best, I'll use "Star Wars" as a reference. If you haven't seen this film, what the heck is wrong with you? Now is a good time to watch it.

George Lucas (the writer/director) knew archetypes, characters and story triggers that would grab a large audience. Most people love this movie because we all respond to the Hero's Journey. It is Universal. We are programmed to recognize archetypes.

The Departure

The Call to Adventure
The call to adventure is the point in a character's life when they realize that things are going to change, whether they like it or not. Often they do not. A telephone ringing, a door knock, a letter, an event or conversation can signify this inevitable change. Anything that sets the hero into motion is his/her call to adventure.

> *Star Wars reference: R2D2's holograph of Princess Leia in distress.*

Refusal of the Call
Often, the hero refuses the call to adventure due to fear, insecurity, a sense of inadequacy or any other range of reasons. But eventually the hero does, or is forced to, take the challenge.

> *Star Wars reference: Uncle Owen reminds Luke of his responsibilities at home. But Luke does accept the mission after storm troopers burn down his farm.*

Supernatural Aid

When the hero commits to the call, his guides and helpers appear. This could come in the form of friends, contacts or any variety of creatures that help propel the hero into motion.

Star Wars reference: Obi Wan Kenobi.

Crossing of the First Threshold

This is the point where the hero actually crosses into the field of adventure, and leaves his/her known world behind. It can be signified by a variety of images: crossing a bridge; driving into town; taking the red pill; a plane lifting off; and so on. A committed hero cannot turn back after this point. The new rules of the unknown world lay ahead of him to discover.

Star Wars reference: Luke leaves his home planet Tantooine.

The Belly of the Whale

The belly of the whale represents the final separation from the hero's known world and self. The hero has separated his/her known world for the unknown, and a better future/self. This phase of story is usually accompanied by conflicts and challenges. Think of almost any movie: once the hero sets off on his journey, he encounters trouble in some fashion or another.

Star Wars reference: The Imperial Falcon is drawn into the Death Star.

The Initiation

The Road of Trials

This is a series of tests and trials, usually coming in sets of three. The first being the smallest.

Star Wars reference: Luke attempts to find Leia.

The Meeting with the Goddess

The hero experiences a love. This is a very important step in the process. Although Joseph Campbell symbolizes this step as a meeting with a goddess, unconditional love and/or self-unification does not have to be represented by a woman or a romantic interest.

Star Wars reference: Luke finds Leia.

Woman as the Temptress

For Campbell, however, this step is about the repulsion that the usually male hero may feel about his own fleshy/earthy nature, and the subsequent attachment or projection of that repulsion towards women. Woman is a metaphor for the physical or material temptations of life, since the hero-knight was often tempted by lust from his spiritual journey.

Star Wars reference not applicable.

Atonement With the Father

In this step the hero must confront and be initiated by whatever holds the ultimate power in his or her life. In many myths and stories this life-and-death power is represented by the father, or a father figure. This is the *center point* of the journey. It does not have to be a male figure, but oftentimes it is. Think about your favorite stories. The character usually encounters a wise old man who helps him with skills and talents that enable him to complete his journey. Depending on what type of story, there could be a variety of father characters. It could be a technology. It could be a friend. A book. A spirit. A woman. A teacher.

Star Wars reference: Obi Wan Kenobi.

Apotheosis

To apotheosize is to deify. When someone dies a physical death, they move on to a state of divine. This is a period of rest, peace and fulfillment before the hero begins the return.

Star Wars reference: Luke becomes a hero rescuing Leia.

The Ultimate Boon

The achievement of the goal of the quest. This is why the hero sets out on his journey. In many myths the boon is something transcendent: like the elixir of life itself, love, a plant that supplies immortality or even the Holy Grail (symbolically, or literally). Whatever it is, it is worth the journey. Remember the "Indiana Jones" movies?

Star Wars reference: Luke saves Leia and R2D2, and then plans to attack the Death Star.

The Return

Refusal of the Return

With all the excitement, growth, freedom, victory and knowledge gained, the hero at first fails to see the point of returning. It's like coming back from vacation—we just don't want to.

Star Wars: Han refuses to return to Death Star.

The Magic Flight

Sometimes the hero must escape with the boon, but not without conflicts. Others want what the hero has taken. The hero will not slip out of sight easily. This comes from the concept of a hero taking something the Gods have been guarding.

Star Wars reference not applicable.

Rescue from Without

A hero also needs guides and assistance in returning. Oftentimes the hero is wounded, or needs a push to start the journey home.

Star Wars reference: Han returns to protect Luke.

The Crossing of the Return Threshold

Upon returning to the hero's old world, he must realize that he has gained knowledge and must try to teach what he has learned… which oftentimes proves to be difficult.

Star Wars reference: Falcon escapes. Death Star explodes.

Master of the Two Worlds
The hero is now comfortable and confident in using his new knowledge within his old world, completing himself fully.

> ***Star Wars reference:*** *Luke and Han praised by assembled troops at end.*

Freedom to Live
Mastery of both worlds enables the hero to live for the moment, without fears.

The Hero's journey schematic is simply a tool. You don't need to copy the form beat for beat. You can delete parts, add parts and re-arrange parts. But every story inherently follows much of the hero's journey, whether it's comedy, drama, action or horror. It's a universal storytelling breakdown of common patterns and characters.

Give it a try. Apply these patterns to any film, or your own script and see what common traits arise.

CHARACTER ARCHETYPES

An archetype is a model from which something is based. The character archetypes listed below derive from Joseph Campbell's "The Hero with a Thousand Faces". They are derived from myths and legends from many cultures spanning thousands of years. Most movie characters can be associated with these universal archetypes. They can be combinations of character archetypes, or only contain partial qualities—but *every* character in a story has at least some archetypal traits.

The Hero

A hero is all about self-sacrifice. Usually, the hero will endure hardship for the sake of his clan or someone else, and it always comes with a price to pay. The hero's journey in a story takes him away from his ordinary life and throws him into the unknown. A hero doesn't necessarily grow by the obstacles he faces, but rather by relationships and wisdom gained from those experiences.

Other characters in a story often have heroic qualities—even villains! A hero may be reluctant or willing; it could be a group of people or a loner-type. They can be innocent, fools, warriors, loners, social— anybody can be a hero. There is also an anti-hero; constructed to be hated or disliked by the audience, while still fulfilling a hero's role.

Mentor

A mentor trains the hero. Typically a mentor is a wise old man or woman. Obi Wan is a mentor in Star Wars; and in the film "Ghost", Whoopi Goldberg's character fills the mentor role. In the movie "The Departed" Jack Nicholson is both a mentor and a villain.

Mentors represent the wise, god-like attributes in the hero. Sometimes the mentor can be inept or foolish but still holds the skills that the hero needs to learn in order to succeed in the quest. The mentor also equips the hero with gifts, tools or weapons that are relevant to his/her undertaking. Oftentimes the hero cannot receive these presents until they have passed a series of tests.

The hero tends to always be very skeptical of the mentor at first.

Threshold Guardian

The threshold is the gateway to the new world the hero must enter. The guardian is typically involved with the antagonist or is neutral, or even becomes an ally to the hero. A threshold guardian tests the hero's worthiness when he/she first enters the new world.

Herald

The herald's role is to announce the challenges of the hero's quest. The role can be a human character or simply a piece of information that shakes up the hero and awakens him/her so that they get aggressive toward their quest. The herald could be signified by an event such as the death of a friend, a riot or bankruptcy. In "Braveheart" the herald is the murder of William's wife.

Shape Shifter

The role of a shape shifter is always inconsistent in their personalities and alliances, keeping the hero off guard. Many times a shape shifter can be a person of the opposite sex, like the Fembots in "Austin Powers". At other times a close friend, an associate or even a mentor in disguise plays the role! In the movie "300" the deformed mutant Spartan shifts shapes and betrays King Leonidas in the end. In "Misery" Annie Wilkes adores Paul Sheldon. She slowly shifts shapes into a psycho who takes a sledgehammer to his ankles.

The idea of the shape shifter can be applied to any and all characters. The hero may even find that he/she needs to shift shapes to get past obstacles. Haven't you ever seen a movie character disguise himself as another person to get into a club, or event? They're shifting shape.

Shadow

The shadow's role is the negative of the hero's role. In the old days, a villain was simply referred to as a heavy. There were heroes and heavies.

The shadow represents the dark side of life, and something the hero wants to rid the world of. The shadow is usually the antagonist. But not all antagonists are shadows—often they just have goals that oppose the hero's goals. And sometimes the antagonist is not a person at all. It could be an animal ("Jaws") a natural disaster ("Twister") or even a vehicle ("Duel").

Regardless of what shape the antagonist comes in, it always proves to be a worthy and powerful opponent to the hero. When they face off, the fight is to the end. The antagonist must be destroyed or be rendered impotent.

Trickster

Every story needs comic relief. The role of a trickster is a mischief-maker. An ally can play the role or associate to the hero, or may even work for the antagonist. "The Pink Panther" is a trickster character. "Ace Ventura: Pet Detective" is a trickster too.

THE STORY TRICKBAG

Below are some tricks of the trade to fill your pouches with. They will aide you when you need tools to work the kinks out, and help you fill the gaps. They are traditions and rules that have been around since the beginning of storytelling. And they'll continue to be around when you and I are six feet under.

Themes

Theme is an idea or topic that runs through your story. Typically the theme is the writer's opinion, which is developed through the character growth and inner storyline. If the theme is too obvious it will seem forced and pretentious. So keep theme implicit in the action with subtle imagery, symbols, metaphors and motifs woven into the story. You may not even know your theme until you're done writing!

Common Movie Themes:
- The great journey
- Loss of innocence
- Love conquers all
- Noble sacrifice
- Greed corrupts
- Revenge
- Fate
- War
- Life is a mystery
- Betrayal
- Courage
- Beauty
- Freedom
- Jealousy
- Loneliness
- Loyalty
- Suffering
- Truth

TIP: *Pick themes you are passionate about. Not something you think other people want to see.*

Motifs

Motifs are recurring elements that have symbolic significance. A motif could be a color, a sound, a piece of dialogue, an animal, a particular camera angle, a pet—anything relative to your story that has meaning or asthetics. There are dozens of motifs found in "The Matrix", including trench coats and sunglasses, black and green matrix code, green hues, artificial intelligence, etc.

Ticking Clock

A ticking clock is applied to create pressure and to give a timeline. If X doesn't happen by Y it will result in Z. Not all stories have time clocks, but many do. They are usually established early on in the film to create drive for the protagonist and to tighten the tension. Ticking clocks are easy to establish and easy to spot in a film. "Run Lola Run" is an example. If Lola doesn't find money to replace the money her boyfriend lost, he will be killed.

Inner Character

Characters have both inner and outer motivations. The outer motivation tends to be the hero's goal. The inner motivation is the human desire inside of that character. Inner and outer motivations can conflict with one another. Maybe you have a main character that is motivated by making money. Well, their real inner motivation could be to make that money… so that they can pay for their daughter's cancer treatment.

Advice: *Discover not only what your character wants, but also what their inner motivation is, which will give them depth of character.*

Using too many characters

If you can develop a great main character, you've done your job. It's tough, but fully developing one main character is a big enough task for a beginning to intermediate writer. Once you start to create a story with a handful of main characters, or dozens and dozens of secondary characters you'll simply lose your readers. The movie "Snatch" pulls off using many characters in my opinion, but Guy Ritchie is experienced and very, very talented. If your name is not Guy Ritchie, learn your chops by working with minimal characters.

Remember, your readers are reading words that conjure images. They won't remember a dozen characters as part of the plot. They'll lose focus, forget, or mix-up what characters are who and what their roles are in the story.

Instead, it's better to really focus on a strong main character and a handful of other characters that are needed for the story. When you think of your favorite films, they usually contain just a few main characters. Don't go for an ensemble piece this early in your writing. Save it for your third script. Learn the basic rules of storytelling first.

Subplots
A subplot—referred to as a "B story" or a "C story", etc.—is a secondary story strand that runs alongside the main "A" storyline. Subplots usually connect to main plots, in either time and place or in a thematically significant manner. Subplots often involve supporting characters and criss-cross with main plots.

Remember, just as a main plot has a beginning, middle and end, so do subplots. Think of them as mini stories inside the main story. You can plot the subplots in the same fashion you plot the main story. Design your structure, pace, tone and characters, then apply it to the main story.

Exposition
Exposition is information revealed through your story. It is needed for audiences to digest the world and truth of your story. The tricky part of conveying information is not to be "on the nose" (too direct) or pretentious. We all know those bad movies that have ten minutes of dialogue explaining a plot point. Those movies suck.

Exposition must be layered properly, and hidden through the craft of screenwriting. Create unique ways to reveal exposition to your audience that won't draw a spotlight to it. This takes practice. And rewrites. Remember; only include the needed facts at the time the audience needs to know those facts. And don't clobber your reader over the head. Be subtle and use imagery instead of dialogue when possible.

Set Up / Pay Off

The term set-up or "plant" in storytelling refers to placing information that will pay off later in the story. This could be written through dialogue, behavior or subtle pieces of action. For example, you could plant a scar on a man's neck in the first act and pay it off in the last act by revealing that he got the scar from a fight where he murdered a victim. Or, you could set up your main character with a special skill in the first act, which comes into play in the climax—for example you could set up your character practicing at a shooting range in Act 1, and in Act 3 they are forced to pick up a gun and kill a bad guy. It's believable now that we remember that the character knows how to use a gun from the shooting range scene.

Rule of Threes

The "rule of three" is a principle that suggests the structure of three. Usually a beginning, middle and end. The concept can be applied to structure of plot, themes, scenes, characters and dialogue. The series of three is also used as a progression to create, build and release.

Humans tend to think in threes. We remember points best when given in groups of three, we scan visual elements best when they come in threes and we like to have three options to choose from. Stand-up comedians use the rule of threes as well. Pay attention to good jokes. They'll hit a punchline, and then go deeper, and then even deeper.

| Some famous characters: Three Muskateers. Three Little Pigs. Three Bears. Three Stooges. Three Men and A Baby. Three's Company. Charlie's Angels. | Examples used in storyline: Cinderella goes to the ball three times. Jack climbs the beanstalk three times. | Odd rules of three: "Third time's a charm." You can live three weeks without food and three days without water. "Three strikes." There are three doors on "Let's make a deal." |

CHAPTER II: WRITING THE SCREENPLAY

The Only Thing You Can't B.S.

Don't let technical aspects get in the way of creativity. Take a deep breathe. Remember, a script should be so easy to read a 10-year-old child can understand it! The trick is simplicity—which goes against everything we've ever been taught in school.

If you've done your homework and come to the table well prepared with a strong outline, formatting is the least of your worries. But there are a lot of rules and techniques that you'll need to understand to make your script professional grade, which will automatically make it stick out in a sea of garbage.

FORMAT SOFTWARE

Don't be a Maverick or cheapskate and format word processing software into a script template. Software can really make your life easier, giving you the freedom to create, e-mail and print professional looking scripts. There are many software makers on the market, just do a *Google* search and you'll discover dozens.

Final Draft is used by the majority of the industry. You can use templates for TV, film and AV format (audio/video) from all your major network shows. The software includes online collaboration features and other goodies. The features are easy to use. You'll be off and running after ten minutes of tinkering around. Literally, all you need to do is press 'Enter' and 'Tab' to move your curser from function to function. All you need to worry about is writing. Prices vary from $99 to $250. It doesn't hurt to shop around. Student discounts are often up to 50% off.

WARNING: *Stay away from no-name software. You want industry standard software.*

LOOKS DO MATTER

Scripts look a certain way. The sheer volume of script submissions makes it so that if your script looks strange or unprofessional it's headed for the dumpster.

A scriptwriter has to adhere to conventions. If you are wealthy and are financing the film yourself, your script can look any way you want. But remember, the cast and crew need a professional script to work off of, and for good reason: scheduling, creating and organization make a film production run smoothly and constructively.

Here are the basic conventions to follow:

Paper dimensions; margins: Use 8 1/2" x 11" white 3-hole punched paper. Page numbers appear in the upper right hand corner. *Do not* number the cover page. The top and bottom margins are between 0.5" and 1". The left margin is between 1.2" and 1.6". The right margin is between 0.5" and 1". *Don't* use special paper, just standard old printing paper. Margins are already set up on writing software.

Font and size: Courier, 12 pt. This is used for timing purposes. One script page should equal one minute of screen time. Don't use fancy fonts. Don't use large or small text.

Binding: Only use brass brads to bind a script. The standard practice is to *only use just two brads*: one at the top and one at the bottom—even though there are three holes. The reason/myth is because an executive will usually remove the brads when reading a script to flip pages easily. It's silly, but it's a common thing. You can usually find brads at office supply stores. If not you can order them online from an online screenwriting store or get them at a local copy shop.

Cover page/title page: DO NOT get fancy here. No artwork. No special covers. No glossy paper. Nothing. It will stand out, yes, but it will also signal that you don't know what you're doing. So unless you're Terry Gillian or Pablo Picasso, don't be artsy.

The title itself: The title should be center page in Bold, 12 to 14 font. Beneath the title should be the words "written by" followed by the author's name. If the story is by another writer, that information should be included by writing "story by" and then the author's name. The bottom left hand corner contains your name and contact information. The bottom right hand corner contains your WGA registration number. That's it. Keep it simple. Script writing software will have title templates built in.

Script length: A typical screenplay runs 90 to 130 pages. Horror and comedy scripts can run short, while dramas tend to run longer. Once you get over 130 pages, you're in the danger zone. Anywhere around 100 pages is a good length for a first time writer. We'll talk about why in the next chapter.

TYPES OF SCRIPTS

Reading Scripts

These are typically spec scripts (scripts written on *speculation* that they will actually sell) or scripts written as work for hire. Reading scripts are meant to be read. The better they are written, the better the chance they'll *actually get read.*

Scripts are read by readers, actors, agents, producers, investors and others. The sheer volume of scripts floating around at any given time is daunting. It's best your script is in the best possible shape. It should read like a movie and move very quickly. There should be a lot of white on the page for notes.

> **TIP:** *Seduce the reader with your format and style, enough to get them to read all the way through to the end. It's a combination of prose, poetry and visual seduction. Don't let them take a breathe.*

Shooting Scripts

You should not worry at all about a shooting script until you go into pre-production. The shooting script has scene numbers, even shot numbers, and colors made, obviously, for coordination and production.

The shooting script takes shape as rewrites are preformed and a collaborative effort is made between the producers, directors, writers, cameramen, wardrobe, art designer, soundman, etc. It is a detailed map, written out shot by shot so that the coordinater and assistant director can break down the script, cast, locations, wardrobe, etc. for scheduling and budgeting. Stunts, outfits, props and effects may be written in caps or in different colors. Scenes, shots and dialogue are numbered consecutively starting at the beginning of the script.

Below is a quick example of what a shooting script scene would look like. The scene header is the 12th scene in the script. The action line on the 12th scene is the 36th action line in the script. The dialogue is the 27th piece of dialogue. Numbers are indicated on both the right and left hand sides of the page.

```
12   INT. BATHROOM - NIGHT                              12

36   Andy kicks the door open. Looks around.           36

37   The floors are DIRTY, walls caked in MUCK.         37

38   A piece of TOILET PAPER hangs from the FAN,        38
     spinning slowly.

39   Andy sighs.                                        39

                        ANDY
27            Wonderful.                                 27
```

Scriptwriting software has options available to develop a shooting script. It's not as technical as it sounds, like anything, it's a process, and there is no wrong or right way of organizing.

BASIC COMPONENTS OF SCREENPLAY FORMAT

There are six basic asthetic components of a properly formated script page: Headers, actions lines, dialogue, sluglines, parantheticals and transitions. Here is an example mini-scene below labeled acordingly:

```
INT. DRESSING ROOM - NIGHT  (Header)

Alice snaps her bra in place sitting at the vanity
mirror, her make-up blotchy from a hard night of dancing.
Joe appears in the doorway seen through the reflection in
the mirror. (Action line)

                    JOE
            (O.S.)  (Paranthetical)
     I thought it was great, kiddo. (Dialogue)

ALICE'S POV (Slugline)

Her face is a wreck in the mirror. Her hands tremble.
Something is off. (Action line)

ON SCENE (Slugline)

Alice grabs her bag off the floor, walks out of the room,
pushing past Joe with a snide look. (Action line)

                                      CUT TO BLACK:
                                      (Transition)
```

"SHOW" DON'T "TELL"

"Don't say the old lady screamed: bring her on and let her scream."

Mark Twain

An important concept to grasp is that screenwriting is visual writing. Good English, grammar and technical writing skills will not make you a good screenwriter—in fact, they will probably make you a poor screenwriter. Good screenwriters *show*, they don't *tell*. They are storytellers. A script is designed to read like a movie…meaning a reader should be able to read a script as fast as it would play on a theater screen. One page = one minute of screen time.

A good way to learn how to write visually is by writing scenes. And reading scripts. And watching movies. Write what you see on the screen, and compare it to how your writing looks.

USE PRESENT TENSE

Scripts are written in present tense from a third-person perspective, or with a combination third and first-person perspective, when using a voiceover narrator. Even if you are writing flashbacks, or your voiceover indicates that the story happened in the past, your scenes on the page should be in present tense as if it IS HAPPENING now! *Do NOT* write your story as if it already took place.

BAD EXAMPLE

```
EXT. DESERT - DAY

John was exhausted as he carried his friend over his
shoulders through the hot day. He was sweaty and dirty.
```

CORRECT EXAMPLE

```
EXT. DESERT - DAY

John staggers as he carries his friend over his shoulder
as the sun beats down. He's filthy from sweat and sand.
```

BASIC FORMATTING TERMS

If you are a complete beginner, here are the basic formatting terms and abbreviations you'll need to get started. If you're an intermediate writer these will be familiar to you. For more advanced options and terms refer to the end of the chapter.

FADE IN: Always start a script with the header FADE IN: in the upper left hand corner in caps.

FADE OUT: End each script with the transition FADE OUT: in the lower right hand corner.

INT. = Interior scene. This is used to signal indoor filming. It will go at the beginning of each scene in the slug or header.

EXT. = Exterior scene. Used to signal an exterior film shoot.

V.O. = Voice over. Used as a narrative tool. VO is good to use for story flow, but be careful about using it simply to solve problems. It's known by professionals as the easy way out. Rule-of-thumb is to stay away from using Voice Overs, unless you're a Martin Scorsese. VO goes beside the character name when using dialogue. Like this:

                    BETTY (V.O.)
            I'm narrating the story.

O.S. = Offscreen. This is used to tell the reader that something is taking place off of the screen, out of view. A character's voice could be heard offscreen.

                    BETTY (O.S.)
            I can be heard, but not seen.

Or, you can signal to something out of frame.

EXAMPLE: Robin turns to the street, staring O.S. Something isn't right, her pupils enlarge.

This technique is used all the time to create suspense, comedy, or plot.

B.G. = Background. This is used in an action line to indicate action is taking place in the background. Remember, visually there are three main planes going on in a movie that creates a depth-of-field perception. The foreground, mid-ground and background. If you need to reveal information in the background of a shot or scene, simply write it in.

EXAMPLE: Tony pays for his pizza. In the B.G. a man with a hoodie lurks at the gumball machine keeping his eye on Tony's kid.

F.G. = Foreground. Used in the action lines. Same rules apply as above.

EXAMPLE: `Alice walks through the aisle. A floral dress steps into frame in the F.G. We've seen this dress before. Pink flower print.`

POV = Point of view. If we want the audience to see something in a character's point of view, we simply write it in caps flush to the left, positioned the same as a header, like this:

```
JOSHUA'S POV

Two men charge us throwing punches.
```

ON SCENE = A transition back to the scene from another angle. Write it in caps as a slugline. Typically you will want to use this transition after a POV shot, a CLOSE-UP or ANGLE ON shot, like this:

```
JOSHUA'S POV

Two men charge us throwing punches.

ON SCENE

A fist knocks Joshua in the nose, hard, sending him to
the ground on his back.
```

CU or CLOSE-UP: A very close detail shot. Use sparingly. Steven Spielberg once said, "A close-up seems like a good idea until you're watching a 10-foot-tall nose in a movie theater." Use it to give a detail, but don't over-use it. Indicate the shot by writing it in caps, on it's own action line. Like this:

```
CLOSE-UP: of an ant, running madly from a nearby shoe.
```

INSERT: Inserts can be used to give detailed information. Here is an example:

```
Mike runs down the alley. He checks his watch.

INSERT: Mike's watch reads 10:00am.
```

```
Mike stops at the donut shop, realizing he has a few
minutes. He looks in the mirror and checks out his gut.
Maybe he shouldn't.
```

FORMAT TECHNIQUES

Okay, now that you've got the basic terms down, lets get more into some rules of the script that will help the writing flow. You want the reader's eye to keep moving. That's the trick. It's manipulation. Dazzle your readers. Make them keep moving', make them keep reading 'til the end.

Scene Headings

Scene headings are written in caps at the top of each scene. Here is a typical example:

```
EXT. OFFICE - BACKDOOR - NIGHT
```

"Ext." means we're using an exterior for production. Office is the location. Backdoor is the scene within the location. And night is the time. So lets say you have a scene in a bathroom at a house. You would use:

```
INT. HOUSE - BATHROOM - DAY
```

Once you have established the main location, you can use shorter versions of headers as you change scenes. So lets say we had a scene start with:

```
INT.  HOUSE - LIVING ROOM - DAY
```

Well, if we cut to another scene within that location, or had a character walk into another room, we could simply write a header—that continues our action, or starts the next scene—like so:

```
BATHROOM
```

We already know we are in a house, we don't need another header. But if you cut to a completely different location, you need to set up the entire header to establish where the action is taking place.

Let's combine those two concepts for an example:

```
INT. HOUSE - LIVING ROOM - NIGHT

Alex enters the front door holding groceries. He is all
smiles. MUSIC plays from the kitchen.

IN THE KITCHEN

A CD player sits on the table. Alex enters. He looks to
the floor. Blood marks lead off into the hallway. Alex
drops the groceries.

                         ALEX
               Mary!?

IN THE BATHROOM

Mary is mangled on the tile floor, bloody. Dead.

HALLWAY

Alex slowly makes his way to the bathroom doorway, which
is open.
```

Action Lines

Action lines are the descriptive lines used after you set up a scene with a header. They describe the action, character, plot and details. This is where good prose comes into play. Remember, the point is to ellicit images through your descriptions.

A good rule of thumb is to keep the action lines no thicker than two fingers in width. I know, technical stuff. I actually picked that one up by a very experienced writing proffesor at USC. It's simple, but it works. The point is that **no one wants to read long blocks of action lines**—it makes your eyes tired! It slows the reader. And that could make the reader put your story down. Not good.

Think of each line of action as a single shot. It won't always work out that way, but it tends to more often than not. So each time there is a new thing happening in the scene, you can drop down and start a fresh action line.

Here is a simple example:

```
INT. COFFEE SHOP - NIGHT

A GRUBBY MAN strolls through the door carrying a duffle
bag. He eyes a blueberry muffin behind the glass case at
the front counter.

He looks around in panic and walks up to the clerk. Sets
the duffle bag on the counter. Pulls a pistol from the
bag and points to the blueberry muffin behind the glass
display, insinuating he wants it.

The clerk is in shock.

The customers stop eating, realizing this guy is serious.
```

Now read the same sample, clumped in a single paragraph of action:

```
INT. COFFEE SHOP - NIGHT

A GRUBBY MAN strolls through the door carrying a duffle
bag. He eyes a blueberry muffin behind the glass case at
the front counter. He looks around in panic and walks up
to the clerk. Sets the duffle bag on the counter. Pulls a
pistol from the bag and points to the blueberry muffin
behind the glass display, insinuating he wants it. The
clerk is in shock. The customers stop eating, realizing
this guy is serious.
```

The first example reads quicker, and burns distinct images in your mind
on a shot by shot basis, more like a film compared to a book.

Using day/night
One mistake beginning writers make is using morning, dawn or dusk to describe what time of day it is in their header descriptions. Don't. The director, cameramen, art directors and coordinator can only work around night and day.

If it's dawn. Write:

```
EXT. BEACH - DAY
```

```
The sun sets over the horizon as a seagull flies across
the misty shoreline.
```

Establishing Scenes
Establishing scenes are short scenes that put the audience into an environment. Think of any movie. Say there is an office scene. Well, usually there would be an establishing shot to show where the office is located. Here is an example:

```
EXT. NEW YORK CITY - ESTABLISHING - DAY
```

```
Statue of liberty. Traffic. Skyscrapers. People in a
hurry. Welcome to the Big Apple.
```

Then, we'd move into our interior office scene.

Character Introductions
Character names are always introduced in CAPS the first time they are seen. Typically, it is good to always include an age or age range for that character, and a visual, but *brief*, description of their character. It is also okay to introduce a character with descriptions that are not physical.

Here is an example of a good character introduction:

```
SUE BARBER, 30ish, rushes into the barber shop and grabs
the razor from the barber before he cuts the man's ear
sitting in the chair. She's a redhead, dressed to kill
with knee-high black boots and a fur vest from which her
breasts are begging to be released. She's also a mom.
Wedding ring on finger. Diaper bag in hand. She's a woman
on the go, balancing life in a crazy world.
```

Don't get caught in the details. Hair color really doesn't matter unless it's part of story. It's all about actors. If you have a character with blonde hair and Demi Moore is interested in the script, then the blonde hair will be re-written as black hair. What you want to describe is a character's *character*—their way of being, their clothing, their personality: the nuances that make them unique and interesting.

Character is revealed through scenes and plot, but it's important to have a nice visual description from the get-go to implant an image in the reader's mind.

Entering and Exiting Scenes

"Get in late, get out early."

When you open a scene, you want to try and START the scene **as late as possible**. When you END a scene you want to try and **exit that scene as early as possible**. I know, it sounds complicated and backwards but it isn't. Remember, we're not writing novels. Pretend your readers have A.D.D. and you'll do fine.

For example, say we have a scene of a husband and wife arguing at a restaurant. Unless you're setting a mood, developing character or plot, we don't need to see them drive up to the parking lot, be seated, order their meals, wait for the food then get into their argument.

We should *get in late* and start the scene a few beats before the argument, which takes place after they've loosened up with a glass of wine. After the argument, we don't need to see them deal with the bill, walk to the car, start the ignition and drive home; we should change scenes and *get out early*, before they even finish eating: for example, we could simply cut to them in bed later on, both blistering mad, but silent.

DIALOGUE

Talk is cheap. Most great films have minimal dialogue and/or very well crafted dialogue. Remember, film is at its heart a visual medium. Dialogue should be used sparingly, and should always tell something about character, or plot. Otherwise, don't use it.

Good dialogue work is a mix of poetry and everyday conversation. When people talk it is disjointed and awkward: cut-off sentences, repeated words and phrases, bad syntax, ramblings, interruptions and pauses are common. It isn't formally constructed or perfectly grammatical—the exception being if that is the way that character speaks (*See the "Speech Patterns" section below*). Basically, you want your dialogue to sound natural, but also have a poetic rhythm that doesn't sound recited or artificial.

Dialogue Tip #1:	Dialogue Tip #2:	Homework:
If you can get a piece of information across without using dialogue, don't use it.	*If you write what you want your characters to say, you're saying it, not them. It will come across as forced. Wait until your characters start speaking to you.*	*Start listening to how people talk. See if you can duplicate it in your writing.*

Dialogue Subtext
Good writers know the power of subtext—or, what is being expressed nonverbally under the actual words said. Dialogue with subtext contains more substance and is more satisfying to a reader and audience.

Here is an example of good subtext from Robert Towne's screenplay "Chinatown", directed by Roman Polanski and starring Jack Nicholson as Detective Gittes.

                    GITTES
          Who is she? And don't give
          me that crap about it being your sister.
          You don't have a sister.

Evelyn is trembling.

                    EVELYN
          I'll tell you the truth.

Gittes smiles.

                    GITTES
          That's good. Now what's her name?

                    EVELYN
          Katherine.

                    GITTES
          Katherine? Katherine who?

                    EVELYNE
          She's my daughter.

Gittes stares at her. He's been charged with anger and when Evelyn says this it explodes.

He hits her full in the face. Evelyn stares back at him. The blow has forced tears from her eyes, but she makes no move, not even to defend herself.

                    GITTES
          I said the truth!

                    EVELYNE
          She's my sister!

Gittes slaps her again.

                    EVELYNE
          She's my daughter!

Gittes slaps her again.

```
                    EVELYNE
          My sister!

He hits her again.

                    EVELYNE
          My daughter, my sister.

He belts her finally, knocking her into a cheap Chinese
vase which shatters and she collapses on the sofa,
sobbing.

                    GITTES
          I said the truth.

                    EVELYNE
          She's my sister and my daughter!
```

("Chinatown". Screenplay by Robert Towne. Paramount pictures. 1974.)

Notice how the scene masterfully covered the subtext instead of hitting us over the head by having Evelyne say that her father raped her? That's how you keep an audience interested; by holding back. Less is more.

"On the Nose" Dialogue

This is an industry term for using dialogue that is blatantly to the point. You'll know when you hear it. It's very cheesy, generic and noncreative. It can take you out of the story completely. Corny is the keyword.

Here is a very good example of **very bad dialogue**:

                    JOHN
        Who's at the door?

                    KIM
        Oh, it's my friend, who was released
        from prison two days ago after being
        caught for stealing a car. The car had a
        briefcase full of money in the trunk.
        No one has found the briefcase. So that's
        why he's coming back. To see if we want
        to help him find the burried suitcase. But
        he's going to need a disguise, our car and a
        passport. I know you don't want to, but we
        need to help him.

Unless you want a "B" movie, take the time to craft and edit your dialogue scenes so they don't read like the above sample. Do you know why it sucks? Because it gives away everything! No subtext. No craft. Funny enough, plenty of scripts out there read like this.

Playing With Parentheticals (it's not sexual)

Parentheticals are descriptive words in brackets beside or below dialogue lines. Typically, they are used to give a character a mood, like this:

                    JIM
                 (frustrated)
        I hate swiss army knives.

You can also use parentheticals to convey "business"(small bits of action for actors) like this:

                    JIM
            (unfolds a Swiss Army Knife)
        Damn these things.

Or, you can use combinations of action, dialogue and parentheticals, like this:

```
Jim pulls a swiss Army Knife from his pouch.

                    JIM
              (trying to open it)
         Damn these things.
                    (frustrated)
         Forget it.

He throws the knife behind him sticking it into the wall.
```

Actors do not like to be told how to act. Only use a paranthetical for small actions, or when it is necessary to get an emotion or tone across for things to make sense. Use lower case. Don't let your parantheticals get too long. Keep it short and sweet. One to three words works best.

Speech Patterns
Each character should have a voice, not only in what they say but *how* they say it. Dialogue can become the rhythm for a scene. You can increase the pace of scenes by quickening the exchange of dialogue and adding interruptions.

Remember, people don't talk like Shakespeare. They use slang, they pause, they hiccup, they curse, they stutter, they use incomplete sentences, half phrases, pose questions as statements and use subtext.

Check out a piece of dialogue from Quentin Tarantino's "True Romance" below. Whether you like his films or not, Tarantino is a master of dialogue and character.

                          CLARENCE
          I'm not eatin' 'cause I'm not hungry.
          I'm not sittin' 'cause I'm not stayin'. I'm not lookin' at the
          movie 'cause I saw it seven years ago. It's "The Mack"
          with Max Julian, Carol Speed, and Richard Pryor,
          written by Bobby Poole, directed by Michael
          Campus, and released by Cinema Releasing
          Company in nineteen-seventy-four. I'm not scared
          of you. I just don't like you. In that envelope is
          some payoff money. Alabama's moving on to some
          greener pastures. We're not negotiating. I don't like
          to barter. I don't like to dicker. I never have fun
          in Tijuana. That price is non-negotiable. What's in
          that envelope is for my peace of mind. My peace of
          mind is worth that much. Not one penny more, not
          one penny more.

("True Romance". Screenplay by Quentin Tarantino. Warner Brothers. 1993.)

CAR SCENE SCENERIOS

Car scene headers are written like this:

`INT. SEDAN - MOVING - NIGHT`

Or this:

`INT. SEDAN - PARKED - NIGHT`

CONTINUOUS SCENE HEADINGS

When jumping from one scene to the next without a break in time, you can transition by writing 'continuous' in the scene heading. Here is a short example:

```
INT. HANGER - DAY

John hops on his motorcycle, starts it up and jets toward
the open door.

EXT. HANGER - CONTINUOUS

John soars out the doors and rips dust down the dirt
driveway toward the street.
```

INT. / EXT. SCENES

Lets say you have a scene that goes back and forth between an interior location and exterior location repeatedly. Maybe we're in a car chase on the freeway and you're cutting back and forth between inside the car and outside the car. You can simply write the header:

```
INT./EXT. SEDAN - MOVING - 405 FREEWAY - NIGHT
```

This way you don't have to write a header each time you show something inside or outside of the car.

Another way to treat this situation is to write sluglines within the scene after you've established a location, like this:

```
EXT. 405 FREEWAY - DAY

Jack's car speeds 100mph down the center lane.

IN THE CAR

Jack opens the glovebox and pulls a gun out.

ON THE FREEWAY

A police car jets onto the onramp.
```

```
IN THE CAR

Jack looks in the rear-view mirror. He knows he's in
trouble. He punches the gas.
```

PHONE SCENES

If you want both parties to be seen on the conversation, here is how you
would handle a simple phone conversation.

```
INT. BOBBY'S ROOM - DAY

Phone RINGS! Bobby picks up.

                        BOBBY
                      (in phone)
            Hello?


                                        INTERCUT WITH:

INT. PHONE-BOOTH - DAY

Sally holds the phone to her ear. She is pregnant and
anxious.

                        SALLY
                      (in phone)
            It isn't good.
```

From here you can just continue the dialogue and action lines without
any additional headers or sluglines until the scene ends. Like this:

```
Bobby fidgits, he closes his eyes awaiting more
information.

                        SALLY
                      (in phone)
            I have to go back in next week.

Bobby rubs his forehead.

                        BOBBY
                      (in phone)
            I hate this. Not knowing.
```

If you don't want the person seen on the other line, you can simply write their dialogue with an (O.S.) parenthetical next it. There's no right or wrong way to do it, phone scenes are a matter of choice, style, flow and combinations of shots, V.O.s, O.S.s, and cuts. Play around with this one to see what works best for your scene.

RESTAURANT SCENES

Typically boring and used way too much. And easy. Try and pick another location that will lead to a more interesting scene. If you do use restaurant scenes, remember to get in late and get out early. If you have to make it a restaurant scene pick a restaurant or setting that an audience hasn't seen a gazillion times. Do some research instead of sticking with the old steak house, café or hot-dog stand.

WRITING FOR EFFECTS

For a reading script, you want the reader to visualize your story. So whatever it takes to get your reader to "see" your story, do it. But at the same time you don't necessarily want to have your script so detailed that it feels like production day or a technical manual like this action line:

```
EFFECT: a ghost hovers around the tree.
```

I personally like the idea of just capping your effects in the prose. Like this action line:

```
Rick steps outside onto the porch. He looks up as a GHOST
hovers around the tree near the top.
```

Later, when the reading script turns into a shooting script (remember, chances are good that you won't even be there for this step) it will be tagged with whatever colors and abbreviations the director, assistant director or effects team decides.

My point is, don't get hung up on technical stuff that you don't need to be a slave to. Your job is to tell the story as well as it can be told. Make it *come alive* for the reader, don't worry much about what will happen during production quite yet even if you plan on directing.

MONTAGES

A montage, or series of shots, is a cinematic device used to show a series of small scenes, all related and building to some conclusion. Although a French word, it was created by Russian director Sergei Eisenstein to elicit emotions. It can be used to signify a passage of time or convey a lot of information within a short amount of time.

You can number the scenes in a montage or letter them.

Here's a sample montage:

```
BEGIN MONTAGE

   1) Baby Tom is born. The doctor smacks his butt.
   2) Tom gets a spanking from his mom on the bed at age
      three.
   3) Tom gets pinched on the butt by a girl at 18.
   4) Tom is all grown up. He's dressed in leather bent
      over a bed getting spanked on the butt with a metal
      baton by a beefy, sadistic gal. Tom likes it.

END MONTAGE
```

FLASHBACKS

A flashback is when a scene flashes back in time to reveal certain information. As a general rule of thumb a flashback jars the pace of a film and is considered exposition. But there are times when it is appropriate, and stylish. Just remember, everytime you use a flashback it's like *hitting the brakes* in a car. Unless you want your audience to slam their faces into the seats in front of them and take themselves out of the momentum of the story, craft the flashbacks carefully.

To format a flashback simply write it as a slugline:

```
FLASHBACK
```

Then write your scene headers and action lines. When you're finished, write another slugline to end the flashback, like this:

```
END FLASHBACK
```

CAPITALIZATION

A reading script is just that: written with the intentions it will be read. So, really, there are no set rules for capitalizations. In fact, some highly successful writers don't even use traditional scene headers or other rules. They write the script to be pleasing to the eye. The Coen Brothers for example ("The Big Lebowski", "O Brother Where Art Thou?") write their reading scripts with as little technical detail as possible. So don't get so caught up on details that won't make your reader enjoy your story any more or less.

It is wise to cap character introductions, sluglines, transitions, scene headings, important sound ques like music or noises and actions heard offscreen.

Remember, using capitalization brings attention. So use common sense. Used effectively, capitalization can create a better reading experience.

GOOD EXAMPLE
Doug falls three stories toward the asphalt parking lot below. THUD! He twitches and moans. He won't be getting up.

ADDING TEXTURE TO SCENES

Scenes need to pop. They need to illicit images. They need to convey setting and character. Bring a scene to life by describing objects and lighting to create mood that will enhance story substance and believability. Set up certain objects in the room to help the scene, whether it is a broken window or rusty headboard in a horror scene, or birds chirping and golden sunsets in a peaceful scene on a farm.

Typically, to set up an atmosphere in a new scene, only use one to three sentences.

TIP: *When adding texture don't overdo the descriptions. Just get your point across and move on.*

TALKING HEADS

Talking heads is a term that refers to characters talking with no action. It's boring. Unless you're Quentin Tarantino you will not be able to get away with 5 to 10 pages of straight dialogue. Even Tarantino's film in the double feature "Grindhouse" was so heavy on dialogue, he couldn't sustain high interest from even his most devoted fans compared to his other films.

If you find that you have a lot of "talkie" scenes, cut them out, edit them or try adding action into the scenes to break up the monotony. If you do have talkie scenes, your dialogue is probably "on the nose" too. Remember, it's much more powerful to reveal information visually.

CAMERA ANGLES AND SHOTS

You are not the cameraman. Repeat: you are *not* the cameraman. It is not your job to determine whether or not you need a medium shot, an angle on, a fish-eye lens or a dolly-shot. For reading scripts, don't overuse detailed camera angles and shots unless they are vital to the story; it slows the pace and will be cut or changed by the director or DP (Director of Photography) anyway.

In fact, reading scripts that contain details in them turn off directors. And what you should be doing is trying to *turn on* directors. Save the details for the shooting script.

If you are working on a shooting script, refer to "Advanced Format Terms" at the end of the chapter.

STAGING: Creating Scene Descriptions

Staging is a term that refers to the placement of humans or objects. A designer can stage a set. A director can stage an actor. A screenwriter has little to no business staging either. But you can give the director and designer a starting point.

Descriptions can work for you or against you. It's a devilish concept. On one hand you must convey imagery and set scenes and characters and write action. On the other hand, you want to stay simple, clean and keep the story moving.

The key is not to overwrite. Keep descriptions crisp. For scenery it just takes a few lines of prose. Set it up, move on. Unless staging has to do with story or character it isn't your job, so don't worry about being anal. You'll come across as a big jerk if you try and micro-manage every aspect of the script by yourself.

EXAMPLE OF OVERWRITING
```
Johnny leans against the Cherry colored Corvette near the
passenger rear door with his thumb in his pants, his left
foot in front of his right, with his shoulder facing the
tree as he looks into the sunset over the plateau which
runs below him from screen left to screen right. Becky
sits in the back, her hair blowing from the wind toward
the back of the car while she crosses her legs. She has
38 freckles on her ankle.
```

CORRECT EXAMPLE
```
Johnny leans against the Corvette looking out over the
plateau at the sun setting. Becky sits in the backseat of
the car staring at Johnny, wanting him.
```

SOUNDS and MUSIC

You can utilize sounds to enhance story, create tension or create plot. You can use music to add tone and style or theme. Sound and music should be written in all caps. For example:

```
INT. BARN - NIGHT

Pigs squiggle around the dusty barn with moonlight
shining through from cracks in the wood siding. A woman
SCREAMS outside.

Begin "BREAK ON THROUGH" by The Doors.
```

Keep in mind that the soundtrack will more than likely not be up to you, so don't spend your time creating it. Song rights could cost as much as $50,000. That's more than most screenwriters ever get paid!

PAGE BREAKS: MORE and CONT.

When you break a page in the middle of dialogue, add the word (MORE) in upper case after the speech at the bottom of the page, like this:

```
                ADAM
    I could use some eye candy.
              (MORE)
```

On the next page use (cont.) in *lower case* to the right of the character name to insinuate that the dialogue has been continued, like this:

```
            ADAM  (cont.)
    It gets lonely in the garden.
```

You won't have to worry about technical stuff like this if you have software, like *Final Draft*. It's automatic.

TRANSITIONS: Use Them Wisely

Transitions are devices that help connect, end, or re-direct scenes or shots. Transitions include CUT TO, WIPE TO, FADE OUT, MATCH CUT, JUMP CUT, FLASH, DISSOLVE. Definitions of these terms are located at the end of the chapter.

I highly recommend staying simple in this department. Don't get cute. It's a distraction to read transitions. In fact, your entire script could be written with no transitions except FADE IN and FADE OUT, and it would be perfectly acceptable. Most beginning writers feel the need to write this--

```
                                    CUT TO:
```

--after each scene. Or they use a lot of DISSOLVES or other flashy devices. Most professionals do not. It slows the pace and lengthens the page count. A film editor will use whatever transitions he/she fancies when sitting in a dark room alone for months at a time working on the film. It's their job. Unless a transition is vital for story, don't worry about them.

Word to the wise: *Just because George Lucas gets away with WIPE TO: transitions in all of the Star Wars movies, doesn't mean you will.*

FORMAT NO-NO's

- Never end a page with a scene heading
- Never start a page with a transition
- Never end a page with a character name line or paranthetical without a line of dialogue
- Never have an action line run longer than a paragraph. Break up the lines for readability

"I'M DONE, NOW WHAT?"

According to Hemingway, "All first drafts are [expletive deleted]."

I think that answers our question.

THE REWRITING PROCESS

So you've spent months, maybe years on your screenplay and now it's time to get it out into the big bad world. Follow these steps first:

- Take a few weeks off from the script. Don't touch it, don't even look at it or think about it. Regain a fresh perspective. Let your fingers heal. Go back into the sunlight.

- Let 3 to 5 people (other than mom) read the script and then listen to their feedback. Do *not* get defensive. Take things with a grain of salt. But if 3 out of 3 readers say the same thing, you'd be a fool not to take note.

- When you start rewriting focus on specific elements during each pass through the script: on one pass focus only on characters, on another pass focus only on structure, on another pass focus only on dialogue, on another pass focus only on format and grammar, etc. This will hone your energies for specific problems.

- Cut, cut, and cut the fat. Typically, a first draft will run 120 to 150 pages and should be slimmed down to 90 to 120 pages by the second draft. William Goldman has said, "You must cut your darlings." Get your knife and saw the fat before you serve the steak.

TIP: *Stick to writing two drafts and a polish. Your script can always get better, but there has to be a point when you just have to let go and move onto a new script while you let the current one go out into the marketplace.*

TELEVISION VS. FILM FORMAT

Whereas film is a visual medium deriving from the era of silent film, TV descended from radio—which means TV scripts, regardless of format, tend to rely heavily on dialogue. Scriptwriting software will give you the option to open a new file template from your favorite TV series, if you choose. TV scripts, referred to as "teleplays" come in many formats. Most TV shows have their own templates and rules.

Types of TV formats:
Situation comedies
One-hour dramas
Half hour dramas
News programming
Talk shows/Variety shows

One-hour drama scripts have a similar format to film scripts because they are shot with one-camera set-ups on location or on stage. Sitcoms are filmed in front of a live audience.

Talk shows, variety shows and news programs typically use the AV (audio/video) format, which divides the script page into two vertical fields where you can see the audio and video next to one another. Software like *Final Draft* will allow you to do this easily.

Sitcom format on the other hand has significant technical differences.

- A sitcom is numbered by each page in addition to scene letters (i.e., "A", "B", "C", etc.)
- The first page of each act of a sitcom contains the name of the show, the title of the script, the act number, and the scene letter.
- Every scene begins on a new page.
- Every scene displays a list of characters. (*Acts, characters and numbered scenes are not labeled in a screenplay for film.*)
- <u>FADE IN</u> is <u>underlined</u> in a sitcom.
- Headings (sluglines) are in CAPS and UNDERLINED.
- (Character lists) are in parenthesis below the slugline.
- Action lines are in all CAPS.
- <u>Character intros/sounds/effects</u> are underlined.
- Dialogue is double-spaced.
- Actor's instructions are inserted into parentheticals.

NOTE: The "Bare Bones Book of Screenwriting" is not specifically geared toward writers wanting to break into TV writing.

ADVANCED FORMAT TERMS

Below you will find a list of advanced format terms for the intermediate writer or those of you working on shooting scripts.

AERIAL SHOT
A shot taken from a plane or helicopter.

ANGLE ON
A type of shot used to signal new information.

BEAT
A "beat" suggests the actor pauses before continuing the dialogue. It is written in parentheticals. A "beat" in action is a pause in action; often used to signify comedic timing or create tension.

CROSSFADE
Used as a transition to fade one scene out and fade into a new scene. Not the same as a dissolve.

CUT TO
The most simple and common transition used to cut from one image to another or a scene to another scene.

DISSOLVE TO
A common transition typically used to convey passage in time.

DOLLY
Dolly shots are moving shots where the camera is placed on a device sitting on tracks.

EXTREMELY LONG SHOT (XLS)
Self-defined. Use only when necessary.

FREEZE FRAME
Used to freeze a frame of the movie.

INTERCUT
Used to signal when you want two scenes or a group of scenes to be intercut with one another. Example: if we have a character that is stealing a diamond at a pawnshop, we may intercut it with the police getting the information and heading out to the scene.

JUMP CUT TO
A transition from one image to the next with a jarring effect. "Jump To" cuts break the flow. Any edgy movie with a heavy drug scene will use jump cuts and music to create a sort of collage to show the effects of a drug high.

MATCH CUT TO
A transition that involves cutting from one image to a matching shot that relates to the first shot in color, shape, form, etc. An example could be a bicycle wheel in the first scene that match cuts to a car tire in the scene following.

PAN
A camera movement used to reveal new information or reveal scenery. Example. If you start a scene on a hilltop and describe the view, you may PAN TO the edge of the cliff where you set up a character, about to jump.

SWISH PAN
Same as PAN with a quick movement. The sitcom "Malcolm in The Middle" uses swish pans when cutting to punch lines in their jokes with a "whish" sound effect.

PUSH IN
A camera move that physically moves toward a subject.

REVERSE ANGLE
Often used to reveal information. If you have a scene where your character sees something offscreen and reacts, you may use a reverse angle to show what he/she is reacting to. It is written as a slugline in caps.

SMASH CUT TO
A transition used to convey a sharp cut for emotional effects.

SPLIT SCREEN SHOT
Used to split the screen in two parts or more to show simultaneous action in both screens. Written as a slugline. To end the split write END SPLIT SCREEN as a slugline.

STEADICAM
A camera device that stays stable while moving, typically worn by the cameraman on his waist. They are heavy and require training, but provide unique shots.

STOCK SHOT
Used to signify stock footage in a script.

SUPER
Abbreviation for superimpose, which signals one image to appear over an initial image. Usually used for titles appearing over scene images. They are written in sluglines, like this: SUPER: *New York, 1963*

TRACKING SHOT
A shot that follows a person or an object. In the film "Goodfellas" the main character is tracked in a long shot where he brings his date into the nightclub. The tracking shot starts in the street and moves into the back of the club, through the kitchen and into the club in a three-minute shot that never breaks.

WIPE TO
A transition that wipes one scene to the next.

ZOOM
Used to signal for the camera to move closer or further away from the subject without physically moving.

CHAPTER III: BUSINESS

A medieval mentality

It's not called Show Art, it's called Show Business. Hollywood and the creatures that inhabit the world of motion pictures and TV intimidate a lot of people. Sometimes they are viewed as mystical, mythical, magical and otherworldly. But people are people, regardless of profession. You'll find good people and very bad people and everything in-between. You'll find tons of ego and mountains of narcissism, but at its heart, this business is still a business. And businesses aren't in business to lose money.

Here are some bare bones survival techniques, tips and tricks to help you navigate the murky waters in an unusual industry.

TREAT YOURSELF AS A BUSINESS

"Early to bed, early to rise, advertise, advertise, and advertise."

Mario Van Peebles

If you have the mentality of, "Someone is bound to discover me," you will have a slow, long and depressing road ahead of you.

You *must* be **pro-active**.

Get business cards. Research. Make calls. Market yourself. Network. Follow the current trends in the market. Know the players and companies involved. Take classes. Wake up early. Go to bed late. Learn. Grow. Build.

Ultimately, your best contact is yourself. No one is out looking to make you a career. It's up to you.

THE BARE BONES TRUTH

If I were Samuel L. Jackson, I might phrase it like this: "This is one cold mother$^%&in' business with some cold mother%^$#in' people."

In my opinion, this is the only business on the face of the earth where hard work, credentials, talent and determination will not necessarily lead to any sort of success, let alone pay your rent consistently—even if you tackle it head on for 20 years!

POP!!

That may have been your bubble bursting.

This should not discourage you in the least bit. But you need to arm yourself with knowledge for the battle.

A great script may open doors, but those looking for a career will constantly have to be knocking.

HOLLYWOOD IS A SMALL COMMUNITY

Look at it this way: fame surrounds itself with fame. Money surrounds itself with money. We do live in a hierarchy society, and its structure is reflected in political, corporate and film communities.

The A-list resources (talent, actors, finance, power) circulate within only, literally, several dozen companies. Many times these are people that have been born into the system, or suffered for years (even decades) at a low level, whom eventually climb up the ladder. Then there are those people with a boatload of money that simply "pay to play". If you have major cash, it's rather simple to purchase a script, hire an actor and call yourself a producer. It can be done in one day.

You cannot live under the illusion that you can just walk into town with a good script and have people kiss your feet. There is no shortage of good scripts, or good writers. That's the reality.

TIP: *Be social. You'll get further with a positive attitude and social life even if you're a mediocre writer.*

THOUGHTS ON FILM SCHOOL

A lot of filmmakers say, "I would have taken my tuition money I spent at film school and made a film." That's one way to think; but film school is a place to hone your craft, skills, talents and relations while in an environment where you can fail without high-risk repercussions. It's better to fail in a learning environment than risk losing major money and years of your life.

I can only speak for myself. I went to USC's School of Cinema/Television after transferring in from a Junior college. I found it a great place to meet people, a time to learn my strengths, weaknesses and options.

Even small film schools are expensive because of materials, labs and production costs. So make sure you are committed and understand the hardships of the career you are getting yourself into.

If you are motivated by income, it's much easier to make money as a lawyer, doctor, businessman, or even a secretary.

NYU, USC, UCLA and AFI are the top rated film schools. If you cannot get in, or do not have the resources, find a film school that you can attend. It's really all about getting your hands on equipment and making films no matter what you have available to you. Talent will rise, regardless of what school you came from, if any.

Steven Spielberg once told a group of USC students, "If you want to be a director, go out and steal a camera, and start directing." I don't think he was encouraging crime, but his point was simple. If you want to make it happen, make it happen. No matter what.

FUN FACT: *Some famous film folk who never went to film school: Richard Linklater, Quentin Tarantino, Roger Avery, Steven Spielberg, Robert Rodriguez, Steven Soderbergh, Spike Jonze.*

At film school you will meet all types of people with different talents and skills. Many of these people will drop out, change majors or leave the industry within five years of exiting college. But the ones who stick with it will be some of your strongest allies in the business.

Will a degree in film or screenwriting guarantee you a job as a writer? No. But it *will* open doors easier than not having one. Sometimes.

TIP #1: *Make friends! That loser who made the terrible film this year could be running Sony in a decade. You never know. Utilize each other's talents. We all can't be good at everything.*

TIP #2: *Work on as a many films in as many different positions as possible to gain experience and network. A friend of mine jumped in as a producer on a short film while in school. That short film went on to win an Oscar in 2007.*

TIP #3: *Make the films you want in school—because it's the last time you'll get to make what you want...unless you're David Lynch.*

BE REALISTIC: <u>start small</u>

Build a foundation. I encourage first-time writers to play the smaller, more manageable game of independent film, TV, low budget film and B-movie markets. Why? Because it's doable. Because you need credits. You need practice. You need contacts. You need experience and you need to pay your dues and grow in your craft.

An agent will have a tough time representing you if you haven't been produced. An actor will have a tough time believing in you if you have no credits. A financing company will have a hard time loaning a producer money based off a no-name writer. You get the point.

> **FUN FACT:** *Embarrassed by the B-movie world? Research all your favorite writers, directors, actors and producers. You'll be surprised at their humble beginnings in Industrial videos, TV, low budget films, commercials, short films, student films, and yes, the occasional skin flick.*

COPYRIGHT YOUR MATERIAL

A script is a piece of intellectual property. *Protect it.* Although you cannot copyright concepts or ideas, you can protect your story, characters, dialogue and details.

"Literary works may be published or unpublished and include dramatic textual works with or without illustrations. Computer programs and databases also are considered literary works."

Put into one envelope or package:

- A completed application Form TX or Short Form TX and Form CON if needed (choose which form to use).
- A $45 payment to "Register of Copyrights."
- Non-returnable copy(ies) of the material to be registered. Read details on deposit requirements.

Send the package to:

Library of Congress
Copyright Office
101 Independence Avenue, S.E.
Washington, D.C. 20559-6000

Your registration becomes effective on the day that the Copyright Office receives your application, payment, and copy (ies) in acceptable form. If your submission is in order, you will receive a certificate of registration in approximately 4 months.

(http://www.copyright.gov/register/literary.html, Sept. 12th, 2006)

REGISTER WITH THE WRITER'S GUILD OF AMERICA (www.wga.org)

Aside from copyrighting your script with the Library of Congress, it's a good idea to register your material with the WGA, a guild designed solely for the purpose of helping writers. You can utilize the script registration process even if you are not a guild member.

If you live east of the Mississippi register your material with the WGA East. If you live west of the Mississippi register your material with the WGA West. If you live *on* the Mississippi river… I don't know what to tell you. But I'm sure you've got a great story to tell.

You can mail in a hardcopy or do the process online at the www.wga.org website. The cost is $20 for non-guild members and $10 for guild members in good standing. Registration is valid for a term of five years.

THE SPEC SCRIPT

A spec script is the term given to a script written on the *speculation* that it will sell. To be blunt, the spec script game is like playing the lottery. There are millions of specs floating around. Even a proven writer, actor, director and producer will have a tough time raising money for their own spec scripts. Let that soak in, *then* think about all the no-namers and beginners trying to compete with them! This is just the reality of the business.

There are a lot of stories about writers selling their spec scripts for 250 thousand to a few million dollars, but this is extremely rare. I stress, this is *extremely* rare. That doesn't mean you shouldn't shoot for the stars, but you should focus more energy on the concept of building a career rather than selling your one-shot script so you can retire.

Look at your first few spec scripts first as learning tools, second as marketing tools. These spec scripts are your calling cards.

> **TIP:** *Before you approach agents, you should have completed at the minimum two spec scripts, preferably three or more.*
>
> **TV Specs:** *If you want to write for TV you must have two spec scripts of existing TV shows. The point of TV specs is to learn the show templates.*

THE WRONG SPEC SCRIPTS

As a first-time writer, you need to be aware that the bigger the budget you write for, the less chance you'll have of selling the script or getting the film made. Stay away from period pieces and huge budget sci-fi scripts unless you are just extremely talented in those areas or cannot help yourself. A small to medium budget script will be easier for an agent to deal with considering you have no credits.

TV SPEC SCRIPTS

If you want to be a TV writer, do not bother writing an original TV show spec. *No newbie will get a show off the ground,* and it cannot be used as a sample since agents and showrunners need to see specs written off existing shows to hire staff writers. The point of writing TV show specs is to prove that you can write for a show's template and characters. You can use your TV specs to market yourself to any TV show, not just the TV shows you wrote the specs for. An agent needs at least two TV spec scripts to market a new writer. Staffing season for TV writers is *generally* mid-April to late-May with work starting on June 1st. Contact the showrunner to push yourself into this market. A showrunner is typically responsible for staffing writers.

WRITING FOR BUDGET

If you are hired to write a low budget film, it may or may not be obvious that you must write within that budget. Use common sense. If you are writing a low budget film you want to get made for less than a one million dollar budget, don't have a helicopter chase sequence that costs $200,000.

Writing for low budget means using minimal characters, locations, stunts, effects and costumes. But that leaves room for creativity. Hey, you could write a pretty effective horror film using three characters and a cabin. Just make sure there's plenty of blood and sex. Low budget scripts tend to rely on good dialogue too.

ADAPTING A BOOK INTO A SCREENPLAY

If you plan on adapting a book into a film, you need to retain the right to the book. Information on obtaining film rights can be obtained through the book's publishing company. Contact information can be obtained through information. E-mail or fax your request to the publishing company's sub-rights department. It may take a few months for a response, which should give you the name of the agent who represents the material. Get in touch with the agent to find out if the book's rights are for sale, option or if there are any questions concerning your request.

LIFE STORY RIGHTS

If you are bringing publicity to highly embarrassing, private facts of non-public persons, you are exposing yourself to litigation without a release. Obviously, it's a good idea to get these rights before you write. But if you don't you can chase the rights down before you take your script to the market. Life rights are negotiable, like anything. You can bet that unless you are dealing with friends and family, people will want money for their rights.

SCRIPT SUBMISSIONS

The quickest way to "get read" by a company or agency is to get a referral from a contact affiliated with that company. If you can't get referrals, then you will need to do blind submissions. Make yourself a budget for photocopies and allocate time for research, letter writing, mailings and follow-ups.

First, research your market. You want to find the agencies and production companies that *deal with your genre*, or have dealt with your type of script in the past.

You're wasting your time and money if you have a comedy that you're trying to get into an agency that only deals with horror movies. You need to target your mailings with accuracy.

You can find agency and production company contact information in the LA411 directory, on the WGA.org website, in books, on www.donedeal.com and a variety of other places. It's easy. Narrow down your mailing list by genre and whether or not the company accepts unsolicited (blind) script submissions.

TIP: *Save money by making the script copies yourself. Never print double sided. Always use a 3–hole punch, and 2 brads.*	**TRICK:** *Create a record of who and when you sent your submissions. Do a follow-up every few months. Don't pester the contacts.*	**ADVICE:** *Never send a script without getting approval by first writing a query letter asking for permission to send the script. If you send a script without a query, it will be thrown away.*

QUERY LETTERS

A query letter is a letter you must write to a company in order to ask permission to send in a script or take a meeting. It may take several months to even get a reply (you usually will), so be patient. When the contact responds to the letter, they will say "no thanks" or they will ask you to send the script and sign a non-disclosure form (see next page) releasing them from any liability in the case that they already have material similar to yours or will in the future. Sign the form. You cannot fight this one.

The query letter should be short, simple, sweet and enticing. In one to three paragraphs introduce yourself and your project. There is no right or wrong way to write a query. You can find samples and templates in screenwriting books and online, but can you imagine the amount of generic template query letters out there? So, I suggest doing your own thing, just be professional. Just use common sense, good writing and make yourself stick out from the herd. Spend several hours on your letter and make it bulletproof. Include a self-addressed envelope with a stamp on it.

> **TIP:** *Ask for a meet-and-greet to introduce yourself. Agents and producers would much rather take a 15-minute meeting with a prospective writer than read their material. It shows initiative, and character. If you get a short meeting like this, don't force the contact to "read you"—just treat it as a "get to know you" meeting.*

RELEASE FORM

An agency or production company will provide you a release form to sign or sometimes (but not often) require you to provide your own. Your script will be trashed if you send a script without a release.

You can view a sample release form at:
http://www.scriptsales.com/ReleaseForm.html

MAILROOM MANIA

A warning: the mailroom in any Hollywood literary agency is a circus, packed to the brim with aggressive go-getters working 12 to 16 hour days at not much above minimum wage. Many burn out quickly. But some do stick with it, make their connections, and end up climbing the ladder after years and years of grunt work. It is *not* a place for writers to start their career. You won't find time to write. This is a place for agents and producers and business people.

The mailroom receives hundreds of spec scripts a day. Workers sort the mail, obviously. Seems simple enough. It isn't. Politics are at play.

Employees are willing to do anything and everything to further their careers. Your script may be thrown out. It may be lost or misrouted. Why? A mailroom clerk doesn't care about you or your script unless it can advance his or her career. They would rather have the agents read their friends' scripts, or a script that has an attachment (like a script with financing, an actor, or director attached to it). Let me put it bluntly; no one is magically rooting for you that doesn't know you or cannot gain from you or your reputation.

NO ONE LIKES TO READ

Every office and home of an industry professional is packed to the roof with scripts. Most of them are terrible, complete trash. Think of it this way: if you were a real estate investor and you had thousands and thousands of people wanting you to look at their 80 page proposals every year, and 99% of them are never what you are looking for, wouldn't you figure out how to screen them? Hence coverage reports.

COVERAGE

A coverage report is a three to five page report on your script, which is filed by production companies and agencies when your script is submitted. Interns and assistants, or other writers acting as independent contractors, are the ones doing the reading and coverage, not agents and producers.

The coverage report contains a 1 – 3 page synopsis and a page or two of personal notes. They are rated with a system evaluating story, style, character, dialogue, concept and marketability. Each script will gain a "pass" (rejection), "consider" or "recommend." Because no one wants to look like an idiot, it is rare that a script is recommended.

It's a system to condense material. The problem is that it could be anyone who is evaluating your material. If that reader doesn't relate to, understand, or simply despises your subject matter, you are bound to get a negative review. But who said the world was fair?

But you can still use coverage samples to market yourself. There are consultants who provide this service ranging from $150 to $300. You can use the coverage in your query letters, for investment packages and to tack onto the top of your script when you submit it to ensure that agencies and production companies have an existing report to look at.

You can visit my site **www.writtenbyclark.com** if interested in getting a quote for coverage, notes or related services.

> **JOB TIP:** *Many writers find jobs as readers to pay the bills while they write. The jobs pay by the script. Typically the low-end pay is $25 per script while the good readers make up to $75 per script. It takes on average three hours to read a script and write coverage. There's even a union for readers!*

MEETINGS MEAN NOTHING (but go anyway)

Your adrenaline can surge if an agent or producer calls you back and wants to meet up. Well, relax. They take meetings all the time to keep their finger on the pulse. Chances are they didn't even read your script—they had an intern or their wife read it, or at the least they thumbed through a few pages. In most cases, the producer probably just read your *coverage report* two minutes before he/she called you. So stay calm, be appreciative, schedule a meeting or talk to them more about your project on the phone.

> **OLD SAYING:** *Don't count on anything until the money is in the bank.*

PITCH MEETINGS

A pitch is a verbal telling of your story to gain interest in your script. It is the preferred method of communicating new material because of the volume of script submissions. Getting a reputable producer or agent to read your script is near impossible.

Practice your pitch to friends and family to perfect it. Only use the best and most logical story components to tell your story. Keep the pitch under 15 minutes. Five to ten minutes will do if you're good. You can use flashcards with notes to flip through, but keep them on your lap and don't look like you're reading off them.

When going to a pitch meeting, dress business casual. Don't think of yourself as a "creative god" and walk in with shorts and a tank top with Homer Simpson on the front.

Do NOT push to get an agent or producer to read you your script. It's a turn off. Instead, just be yourself, tell them what you are working on and see what type of projects they have in the works.

Don't put on a dog and pony show. Be exciting, but not annoying. You can use visual materials if it works, such as drawings, video, pictures, articles, etc. Keep the pace moving. The key is to entertain your audience.

> **TIPS:** *Be on time. Be nice to everyone, including the secretary. Have a smile on. Your best approach is to be humble, confident and memorable.*

SCREENPLAY CONTESTS & FELLOWSHIPS

Anyone can run a screenplay contest. You create a company, advertise, hire readers (to be legit), charge writers a submission fee, choose a winner, give away a small prize or free service—and that's that. It's become a business in many cases. Your script probably isn't even being read. And if it is, interns are reading it! Someone with less experience than you.

Still, contests can be a great venue for exposure and even better motivation to complete projects. Stick with the well-known contests like Disney Fellowship, Nichols, Zoetrope, Slamdance and Sundance Lab. Allocate a budget for yourself. Typical entry fees range from $40 to $60.

Placing high or low in a contest does not determine your career as a writer or measure your talents or skills. Remember, writing is very subjective. Your readers may not understand the tone, hate the subject matter or not relate to your story. Your readers may not even read more than the first ten pages of the script. There are many reasons. Plenty of working professionals don't place well in contests. Take any results, even wins, with a grain of salt.

> **TIP:** *Submit your scripts and move on. Deal with rejection or acceptance once it comes. It's a numbers game.*

PITCH FESTS

Pitch fests are events where writers pay a fee (up to $500) to pitch their scripts to agents or producers. Sounds good. Well don't jump up and down. Always remember that this is a business. Although some pitch fests are going to be legit, some will not be. The big name companies putting these on will typically send their interns and assistants to these events as representatives, and give them titles like Jr. Executives and associates. See the illusion? You pay a fee and you're pitching to interns! Well, not to say it couldn't work. Maybe an assistant would like your script and pass it along to his or her boss. But, chances are *they will not*. An assistant or intern is going to be very selective. If they refer something to their boss that's bad it makes *them* look like jerks. It's much easier to just say "no."

> **TIP:** *Do your research. Find out who will be there. Target your approach.*

THE SCRIPT OPTION EXPLAINED

An option is the exclusive right, usually obtained for a fee, to buy or sell something within a specified time at a set price.

The concept of optioning a screenplay is the same as optioning a stock. A buyer offers a fee to hold the rights to the property for a set amount of time with the option to buyout.

Why would producers be interested in optioning a script rather than buying it? It's cheaper. Producers typically secure funds for their films. They do not want to take a chance and pay a large amount of money (if they even have the money) to buy a script that may never become a movie, or may take five years to come together. Why bother, when they can pay a small upfront fee to reserve the rights to the movie while they raise money for it. The risk is low.

Typical option lengths are 6 months, 12 months and 18 months. The money varies as much as a purchase price. If you're a first-time writer, and you're good, most producers will only offer you an option fee ranging from $1.00 (yes, a buck) to maybe a few thousand dollars.

It is not uncommon even for a producer at a large studio to offer such a small option payment. So don't be offended quite yet. Many writers make a living purely off option fees. Their work may never see the light of day. But they can pay rent and eat. Barely.

Remember, once you sign an option contract you can't take that script and shop it around to other producers. Once you're optioned, you have no control until the option runs out. So be selective about an option agreement. If you need the money, $500 to $5,000 is a good payment for a no-name writer. If you have no other opportunities on your lap and a producer offers to option your script for $1.00, I suggest taking it. The point is to build your name, get credits and get your scripts produced so that you have leverage.

WORK FOR HIRE

"You call this a script? Give me a couple of $5,000-a-week writers and I'll write it myself."

Joe Pasternak, producer

A "work for hire" is when you get paid to write a script which is based off someone else's ideas or when you rewrite another writer's work. It is very, very, very common, and is actually the quickest way to shotgun your career as a fresh writer. Usually a producer, actor or director will have an idea, treatment or draft of a movie, but will not have the skill, talent or time to put it to paper.

Your best shot as a new writer is to land a small assignment on an independent project rewriting a script to make it better or taking a producer's half-baked treatment and turning it into a tangible script. You'll be paid and, hopefully, get at least a shared credit.

In order to get these assignments you must prove that you can handle the material. This is where having your spec scripts will come in handy.

NEGOTIATING FOR BEGINNERS

If you are non-union, your rates, needs and wants, like most things in life, are negotiable. When negotiating you must learn what leverage you have. Do you have credentials? Schooling? Do you have a special talent, style or knowledge for the project? Are you stellar but haven't had a break yet? Or does the producer's wife owe you a favor? Use what you've got.

Most producers look for writers that have something in common with the material. So if you're an ex-jockey, you're going to have a helluva better shot at getting hired to write a horse racing film than you would a film about wrestling.

Upfront Rates:
A typical upfront rate for a work for hire from scratch is 2% to 3% of the production budget. So if your producer has $250,000 to make a low budget film, it would be acceptable for him/her to pay the writer $2,500 to $5,000 for writing services.

Production bonus:
You can negotiate a starter fee (initial payment) with a production bonus, meaning you will get paid another lump sum if/when the film actually begins production.

Deferment:
Deferment is something you'll hear often as a new writer. Run away! Producers will try and get you to work for free upfront, while deferring the payment until after the film is made. The problem here is that if the producer cannot pay you anything upfront, that means chances are they do not have the financing. Which means, they may never have the financing. Which means your work may be in vain.

Even if the producer does raise the money and make the film, you more than likely will never see the promised deferment because of how a film recoups money. First of all, a film's budget is only half the costs. Marketing budgets typically match the production budget. Most films only break even after years of revenue from DVD sales and rentals. You can easily be lost in the shuffle, manipulated, and ripped-off. But chances are, there will be no money to distribute to the writer.

Credit:
Make sure that you get the credit you deserve. Credits apply toward your Guild eligibility and give you power to bring to the table with your next job. There are several credits you can fight for:

- Story by
- Created by
- Written By
- Screenplay by
- Teleplay by
- Story and Screenplay by
- Based on the idea by

Royalties (a.k.a. backend points):
Royalties are dividends paid after initial investments have been paid off from a film. As a rule of thumb, you'll never see royalties unless you're involved in a huge hit, or a moderate success from a low budget. If a film breaks even from production and marketing costs it is in a way considered a success. So, negotiating royalties should not be a high priority for you, even though it sounds appealing. A typical percentage for a writer that can negotiate royalties is 2.5% to 5% of net profits. If you have a franchise on your hands, you will retire early.

BECOMING A MEMBER OF THE WGA

Membership to the Writers Guild of America is granted based off of a system of units, or credits. In order to be eligible for current membership a writer must acquire a minimum of 24 units in the 3 years preceding application. An initiation fee of $2,500 is due upon acceptance.

SCHEDULE OF UNITS OF CREDIT

Two Units
For each complete week of employment within the Guild's jurisdiction on a week-to-week basis.

Three Units
Story for a radio or television program less than 30 minutes shall be prorated in increments of 10 minutes or less.

Four Units
Story for a short subject theatrical motion picture of any length or for a radio or television program or breakdown for a non-primetime serial 30 minutes through 60 minutes.

Six Units
Teleplay or radio play less than 30 minutes shall be prorated in 5-minute increments; Television format for a new serial or series; "Created By" credit given pursuant to the separation of rights provisions of the WGA Theatrical and Television Basic Agreement in addition to other units accrued for the literary material on which the "Created By" credit is based.

Eight Units
Story for a radio or television program or breakdown for a non-primetime serial more than 60 minutes and less than 90 minutes; Screenplay for a short subject theatrical motion picture or for a radio play or teleplay 30 minutes through 60 minutes.

12 Units
Story for a radio or television program 90 minutes or longer or story for a feature-length theatrical motion picture; or breakdown for a non-primetime serial 90 minutes or longer. Radio play or teleplay more than 60 minutes and less than 90 minutes.

24 Units
Screenplay for a feature-length theatrical motion picture; radio play or teleplay 90 minutes or longer; Long-term story projection, which is defined for this purpose as a bible, for a specified term, on an existing, five times per week non-prime time serial; Bible for any television serial or primetime miniseries of at least four hours.

A Rewrite
One-half the number of units allotted to the applicable category of work.

A Polish
One-quarter the number of units allotted to the applicable category of work.

An Option
One-half the number of units allotted to the applicable category of work subject to a maximum entitlement of eight such units per project in any one year. An extension or renewal of the same option shall not be accorded additional units. If an option on previously unexploited literary material is exercised, the sale of this material is accorded the number of units applicable to the work minus the number of units accorded to the option of the same material.

(http://www.wga.org/subpage_whoweare.aspx?id=84, June 21st 2006)

WGA MINIMUMS

Once you're in the guild there is a very decent pay scale that will make up for all the suffering you did along the way.

The breakdown can be downloaded in a PDF file from:
http://www.wga.org/subpage_writersresources.aspx?id=68

If you get into the guild, you are not allowed to work on non-union projects. But you'll have access to the best resources in the screenwriting community.

I bid you adou,

- Josh

USEFUL BUSINESS TERMS

Against: A fee is paid upfront as a down payment towards a final and total sum of money. The difference is paid at a later date.

Attached: When an actor, director or producer agrees to be involved in a screenplay.

Creative exec: A person involved in deciding if a script is valuable to the company. They will more than likely be involved in development.

Development: The process of developing an idea, treatment or story into a script. Little money flows through development departments, which makes them the low-end paying part of the industry. Most projects never come out of development, which is why it is often referred to as *development hell.*

First look deal: When an individual or company must allow a studio the first right of refusal on purchasing and or producing a project.

Green light: When a script is given approval to move out of development and into production.

Heat: A term referring to a project that generates much interest, therefore demands a large purchase price.

Indie: Short for independent. Refers to a film or company that works outside of the Hollywood system.

MOW: Movie of the Week. Movies made directly for TV.

Notes: Comments and feedback on creative property.

Package: Collection of elements attached to a script put together by an agency or a production company. This increases the chances of selling the project.

Page one (rewrite): A complete overhaul of a script.

Polish: A re-write of a script that typically includes dialogue work, character work, slimming the budget, etc.

Property: A script, book or piece of literary property.

Signatory: A production company or studio that is a member of the guilds and must adhere to structures.

Solicited: When an agent or producer requests a script by a writer or producer.

Track: Refers to following the progress of a project.

Trade (trade papers): Daily periodicals. The main trades are "The Hollywood Reporter" and "Variety"magazines.

Turnaround: If a project is not produced in a certain amount of time, the script will be offered to other buyers. This makes a project less attractive.

Unsolicited: A script sent out without a request by phone or mail to a producer or agency. These scripts will be trashed.

INDEX

BIBLIOGRAPHY

Breimer, Stephen F. "The Screenwriter's Legal Guide", Allworth, 2nd edition, 1999.

Campbell, Joseph. "The Hero with a Thousand Faces", Bolligen Series, New Jersey, 3rd printing, Princeton University Press, 1973.

Goldman, William. "Which Lie Did I Tell?", Pantheon, 2000.

McKee, Robert. "Story: Substance, Structure, Style and the Principles of Screenwriting", Harper Collins, 1997.

Suppa, Ron. "This Business of Screenwriting", Lone Eagle Publishing, 1999.

Towne, Robert. "Chinatown" screenplay. Paramount pictures, 1974.

Tarantino, Quentin. "True Romance", Warner Brothers. 1993.

Volger, Christopher. "The Writer's Journey: Mythic Structure for Storytellers and Screenwriters", California: Michael Wiese productions, 1992.

INTERNET BIBLIOGRAPHY

"Copyright" (As of Sept. 12th, 2006):
www.copyright.gov/register/literary.html

Done Deal:
www.scriptsales.com

Drew's Script-o-Rama:
www.script-o-rama.com

Hollywood Literary Sales:
hollywoodlitsales.com

"Release Form" (As of Feb. 2006):
www.scriptsales.com/ReleaseForm.html

"Structure and Plot" (As of Feb. 11, 2007):
www.musik-therapie.at/PederHill/Structure&Plot.htm

"Synopsis: The Player." (As of Jan. 2 2007):
movies.aol.com/movie/the-player/6330/synopsis

"WGA Schedule of Units." (As of Feb 2, 2007):
www.wga.org/subpage_whoweare.aspx?id=84

ISBN-13: 978-0-9795102-0-5

CPSIA information can be obtained
at www.ICGtesting.com
Printed in the USA
LVHW021706240121
677365LV00009B/582

9 780979 510205